Mandala
COLOURING BOOK

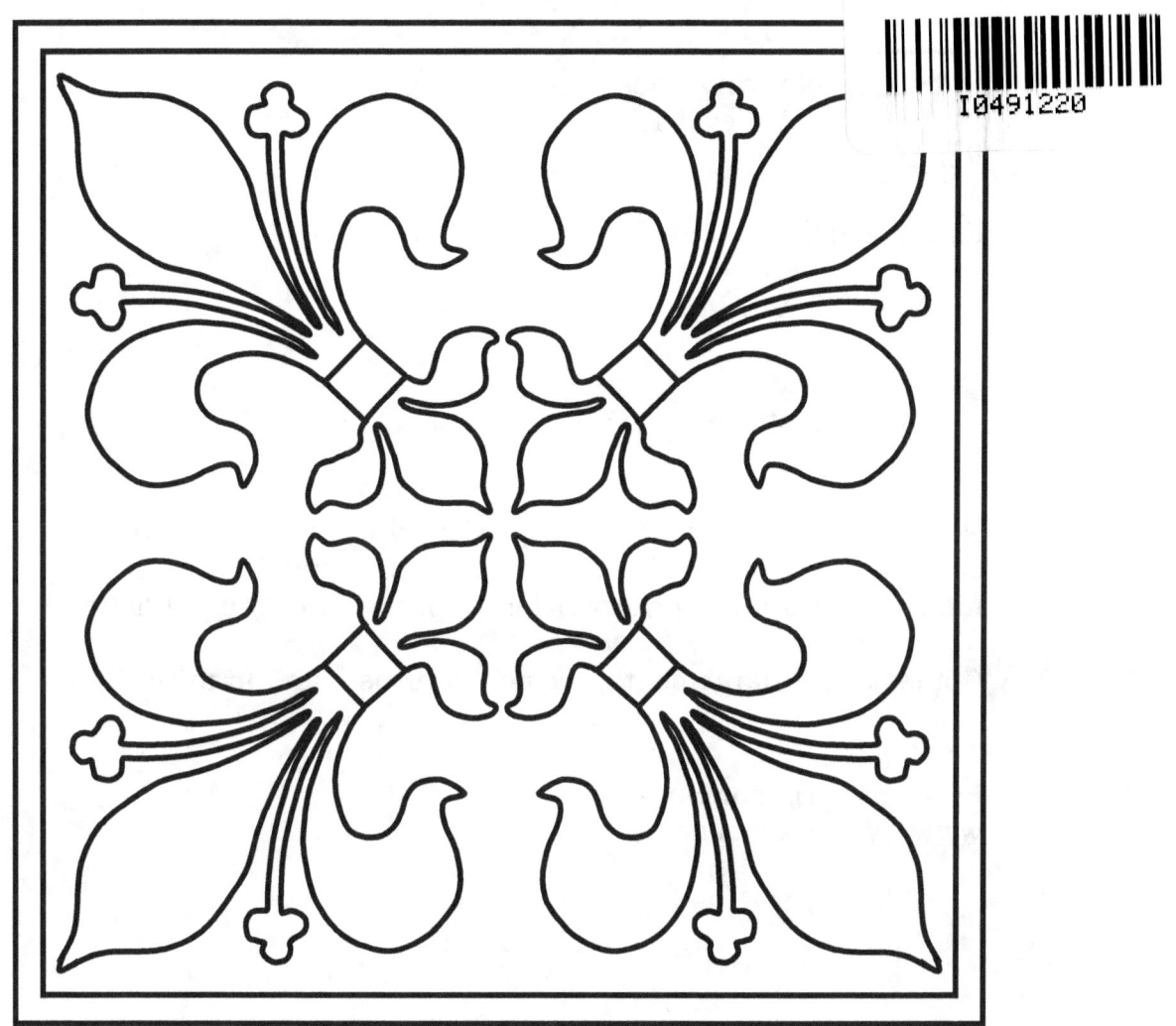

Inspired by Medieval Tiles Vol. 2
Sharla Race

Mandala Colouring Book
Inspired by Medieval Tiles
Vol. 2

First published in 2013 by Tigmor Books.

ISBN: 978-1-907119-21-7

Publisher: Tigmor Books
www.tigmorbooks.co.uk

Welcome

All the mandalas in this colouring book are, in one way or another, based on medieval tiles found at abbeys, priories, churches, and cathedrals in the UK.

The designs on these medieval tiles varies enormously from the incredibly plain and simple to the more ornate and complex. The various ways in which the tiles were arranged to form vast pavements meant that even the most simple tiles could be used to form complex patterns.

Each tile design is a mini work of art—medieval man, just like twenty first century man, expressed his creativity in art and sculpture and the tiles we have remaining are all examples of this. Very few tiles can now be viewed in situ but we are fortunate that many have been preserved by museums and heritage organisations.

I adore looking at these designs and being inspired by them. Sometimes I replicate the design exactly but more generally I use the designs as a starting point to create a unique mandala.

It is my wish that you experience as much joy colouring these mandalas as I had creating them.

Sharla Race

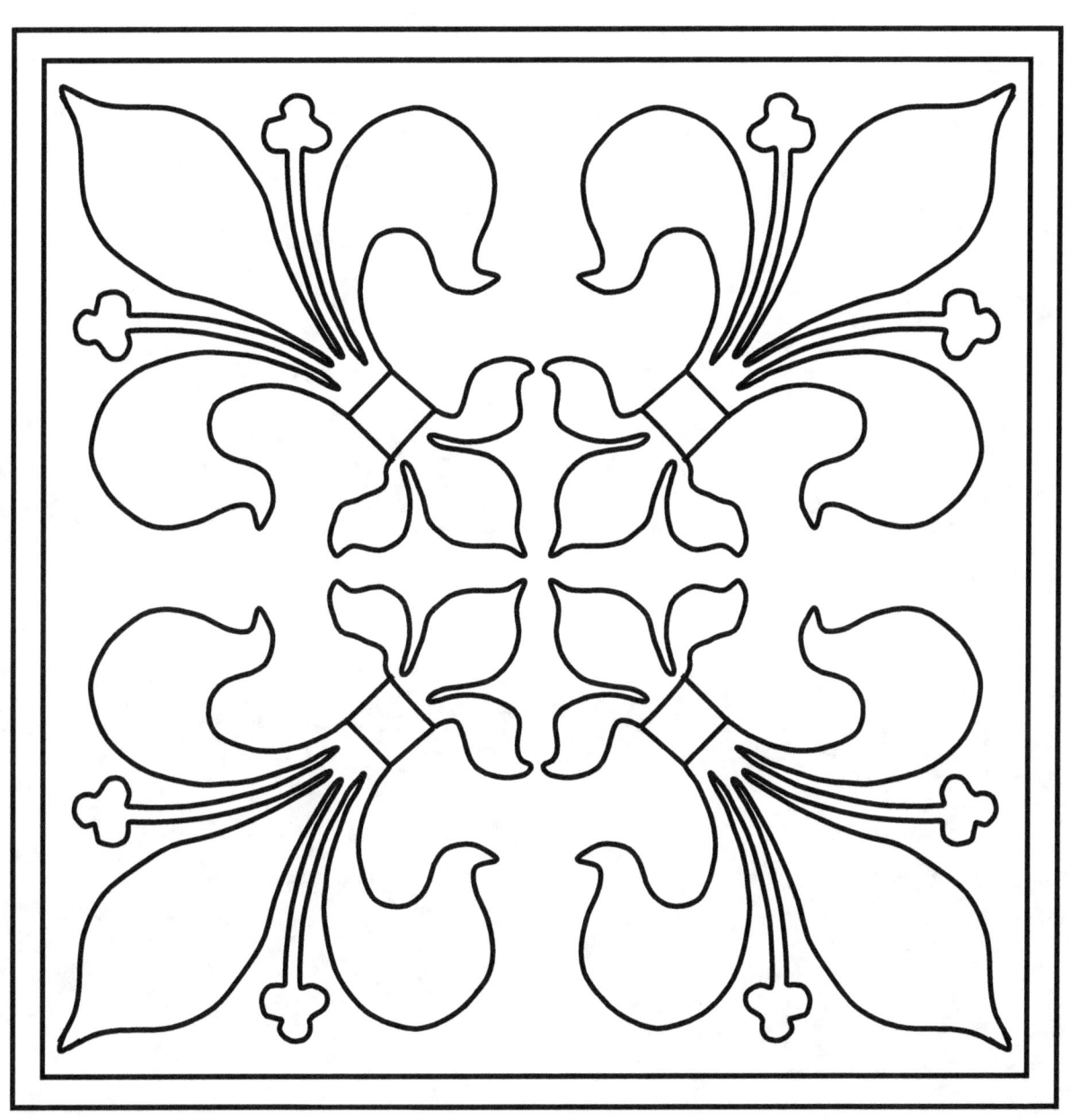

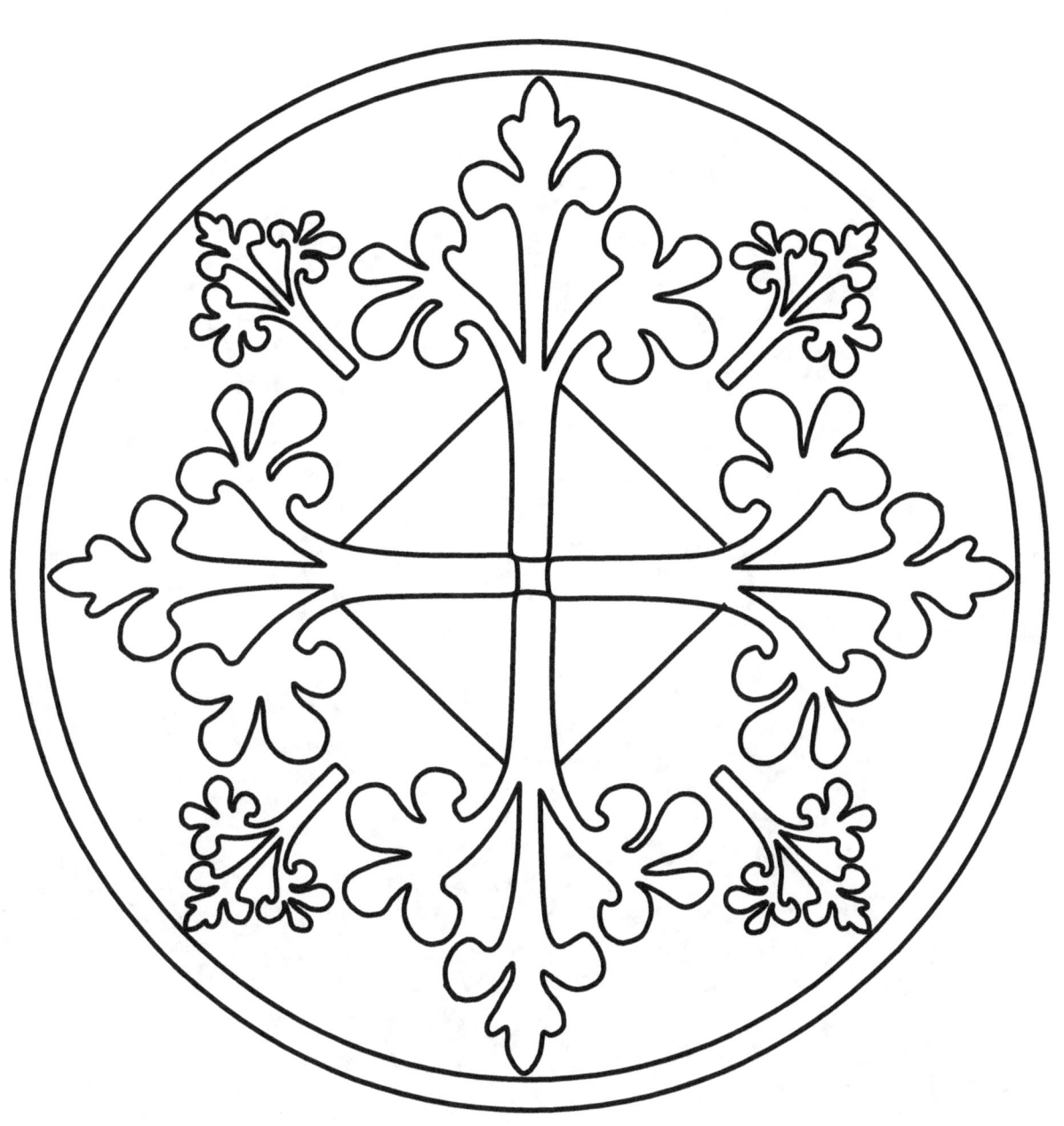

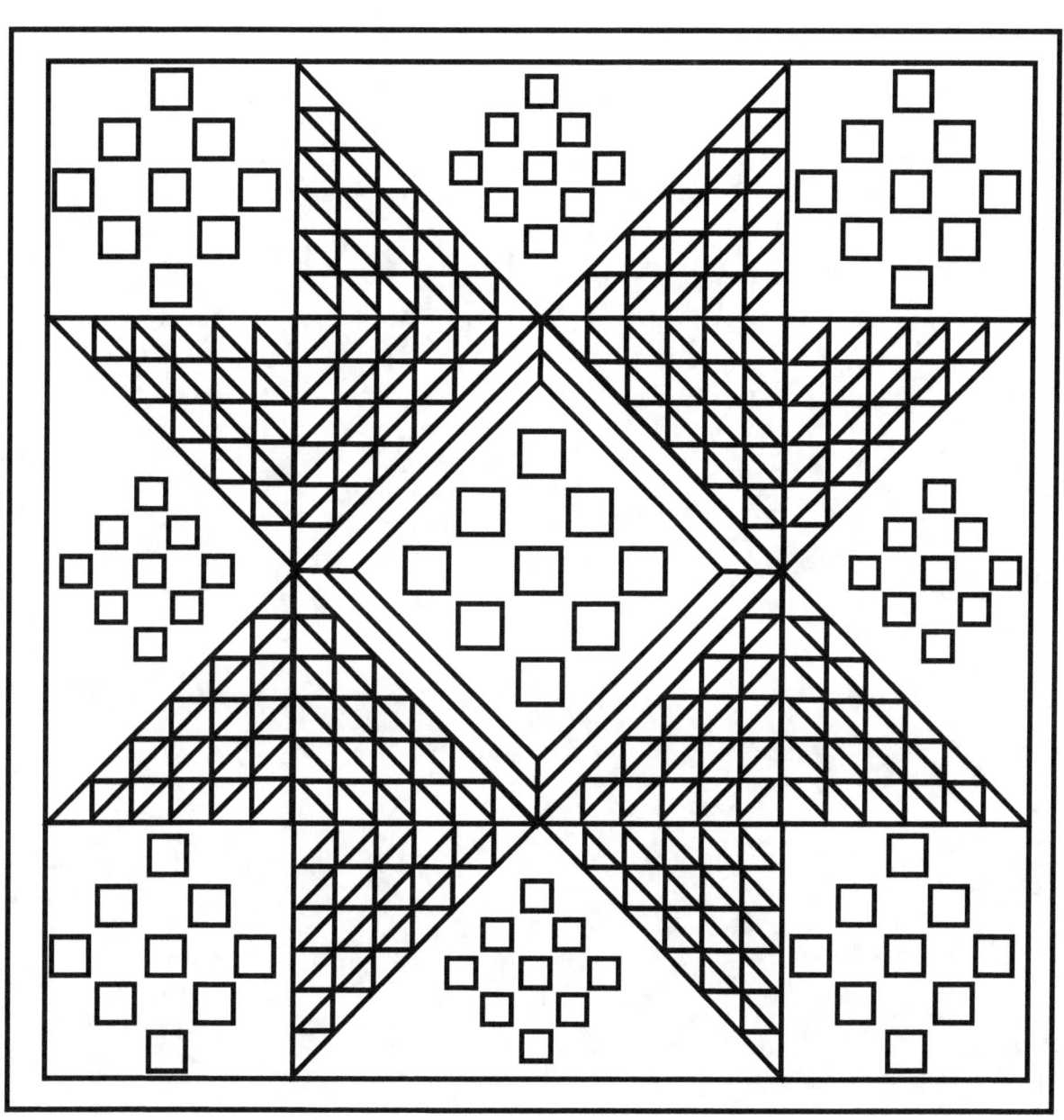

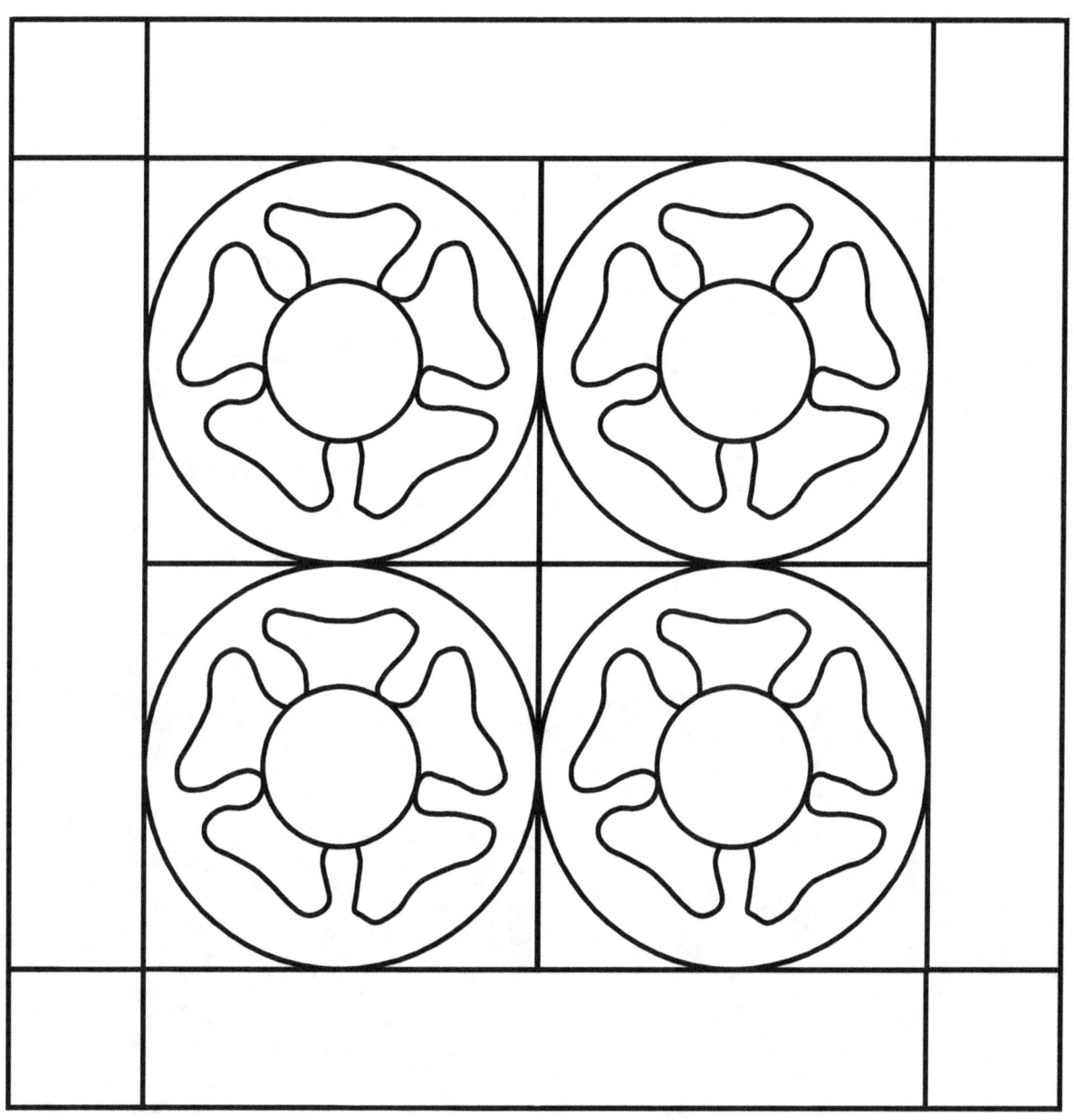

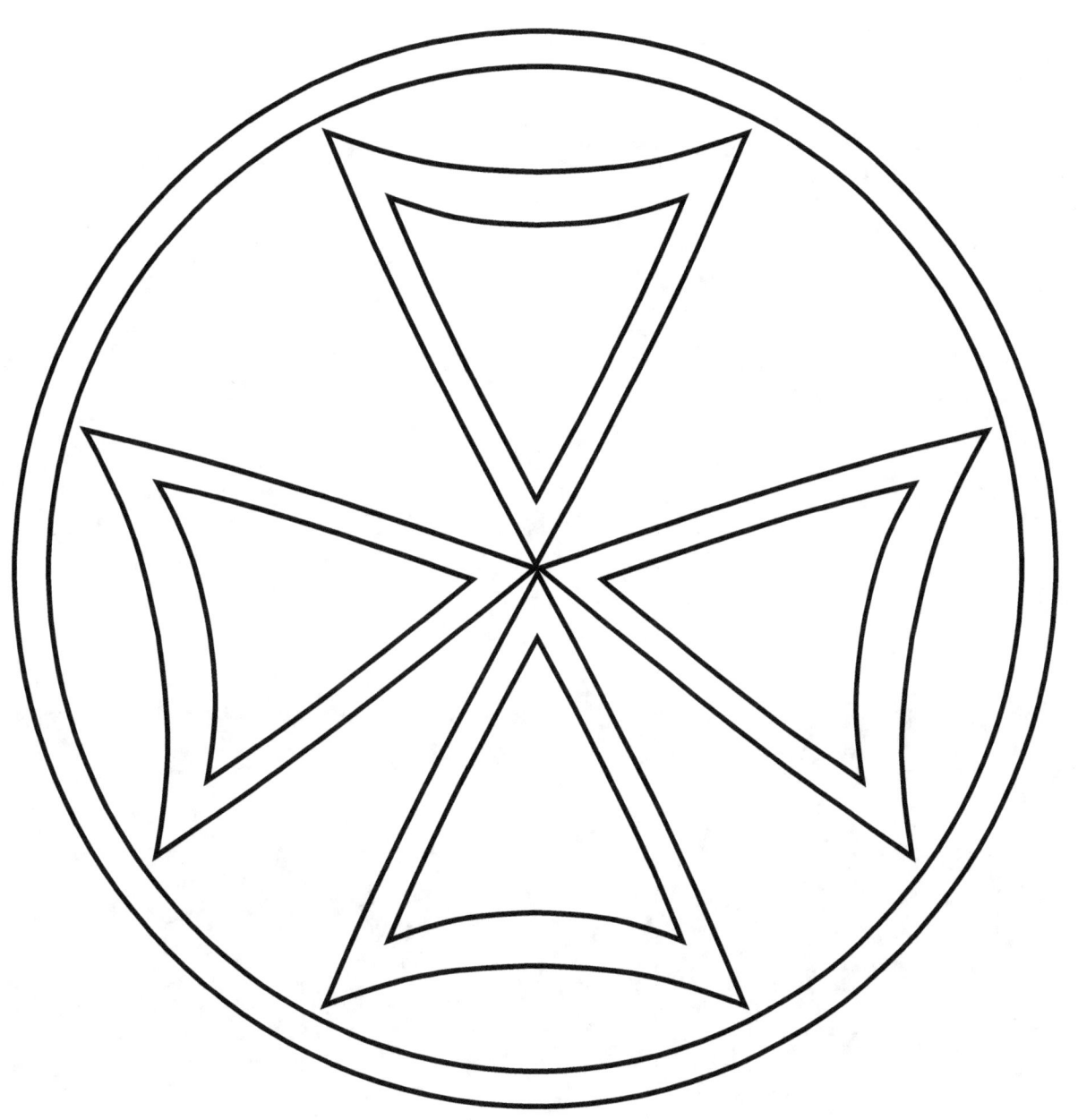

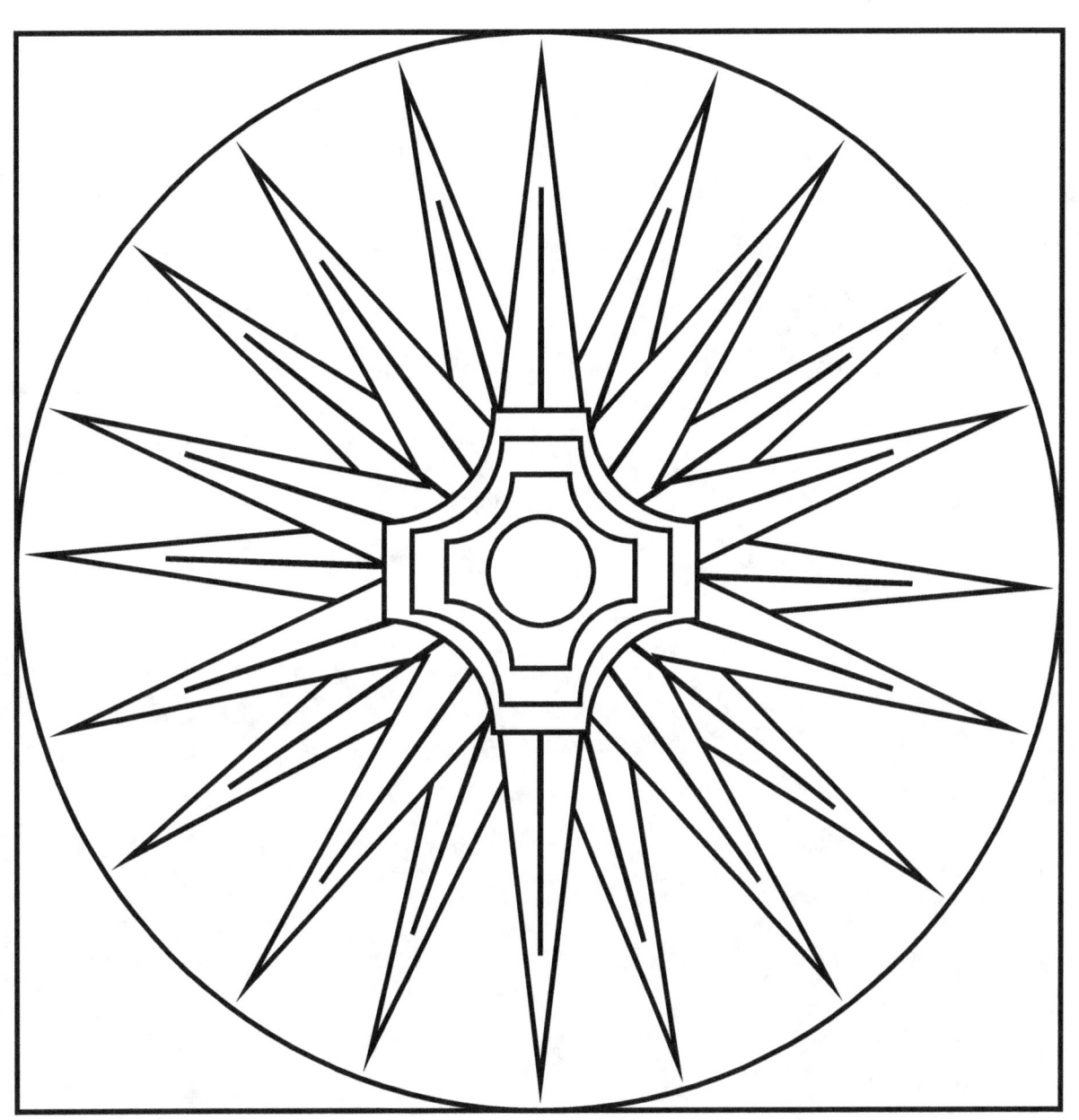

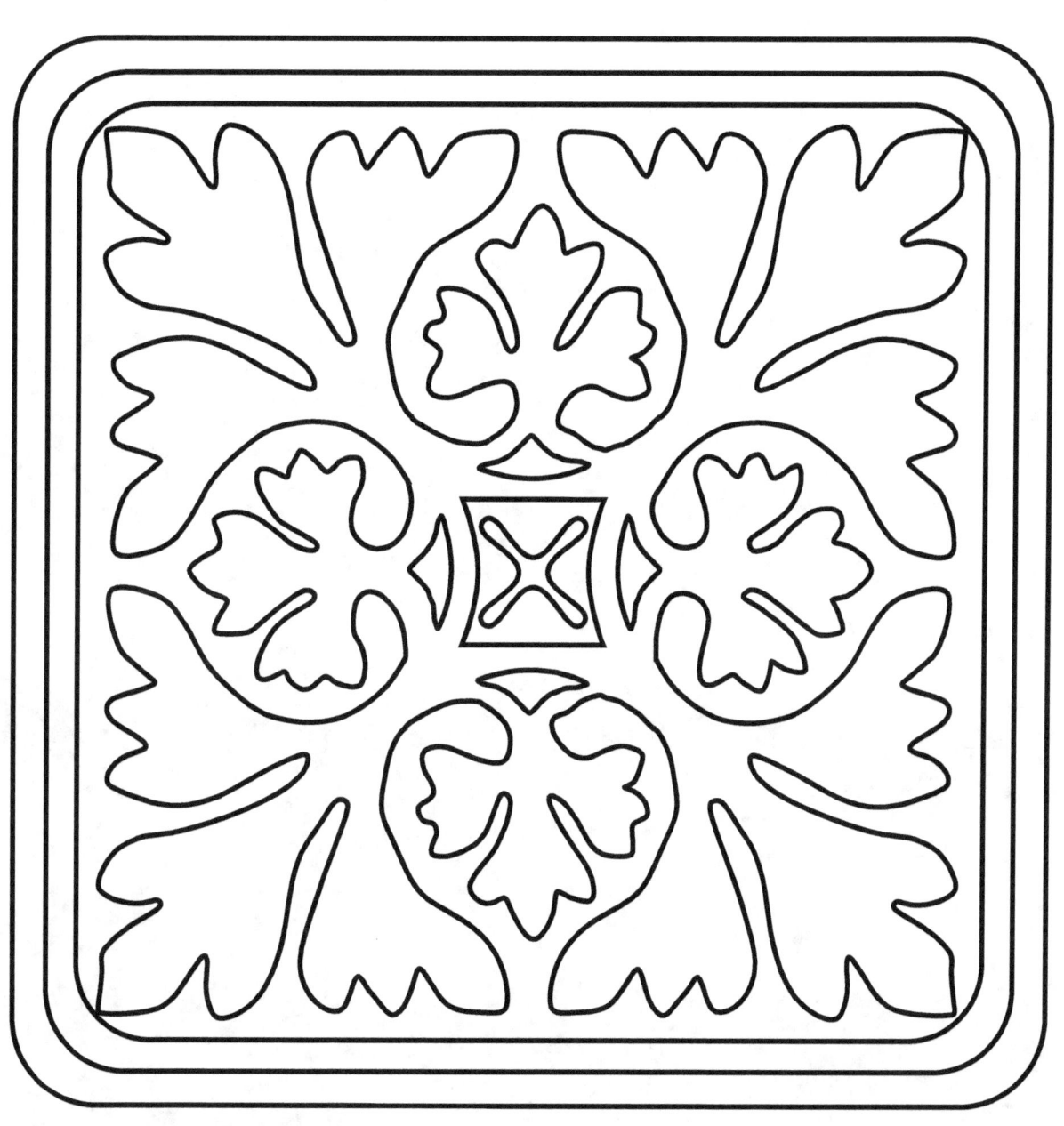

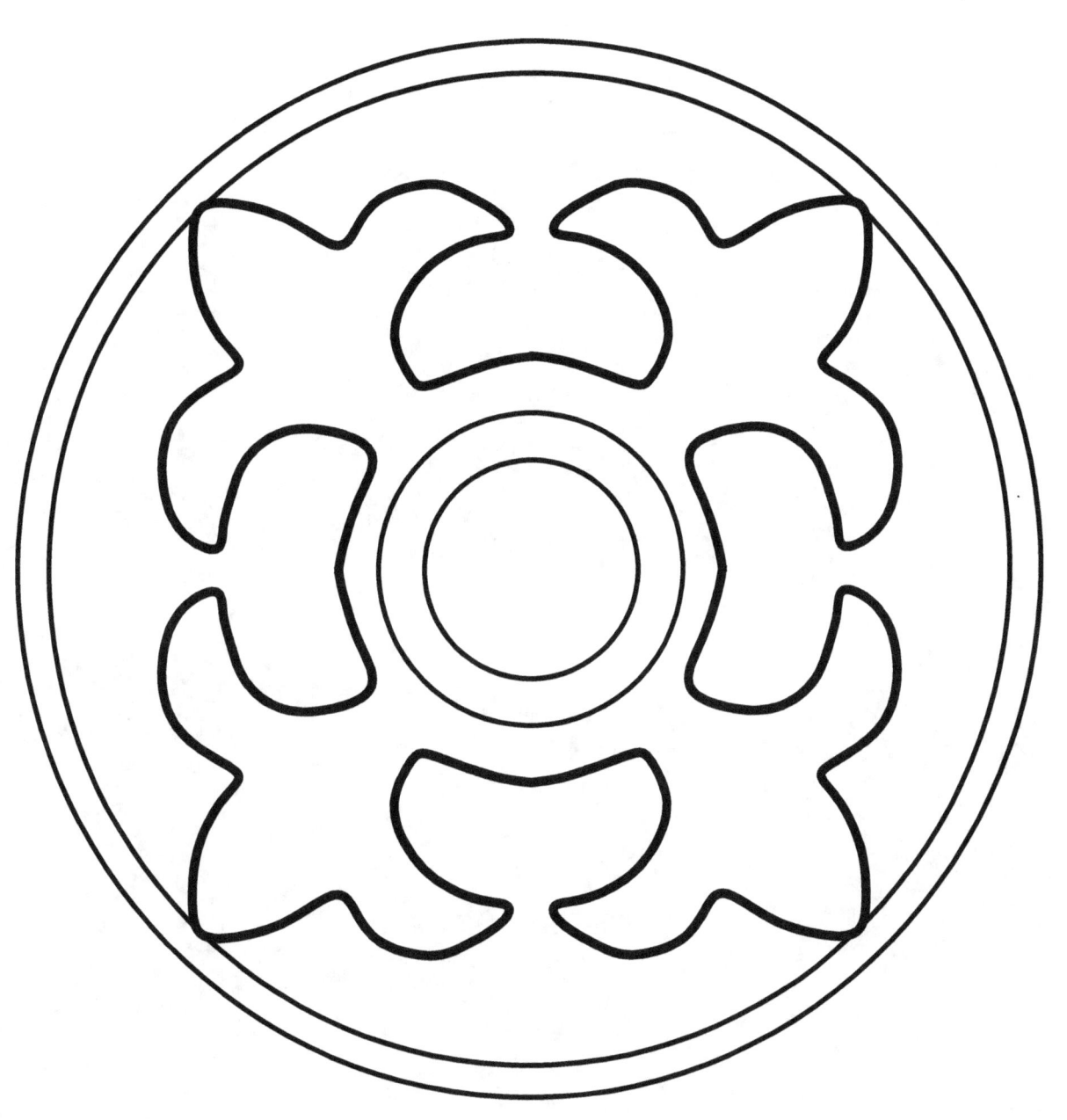

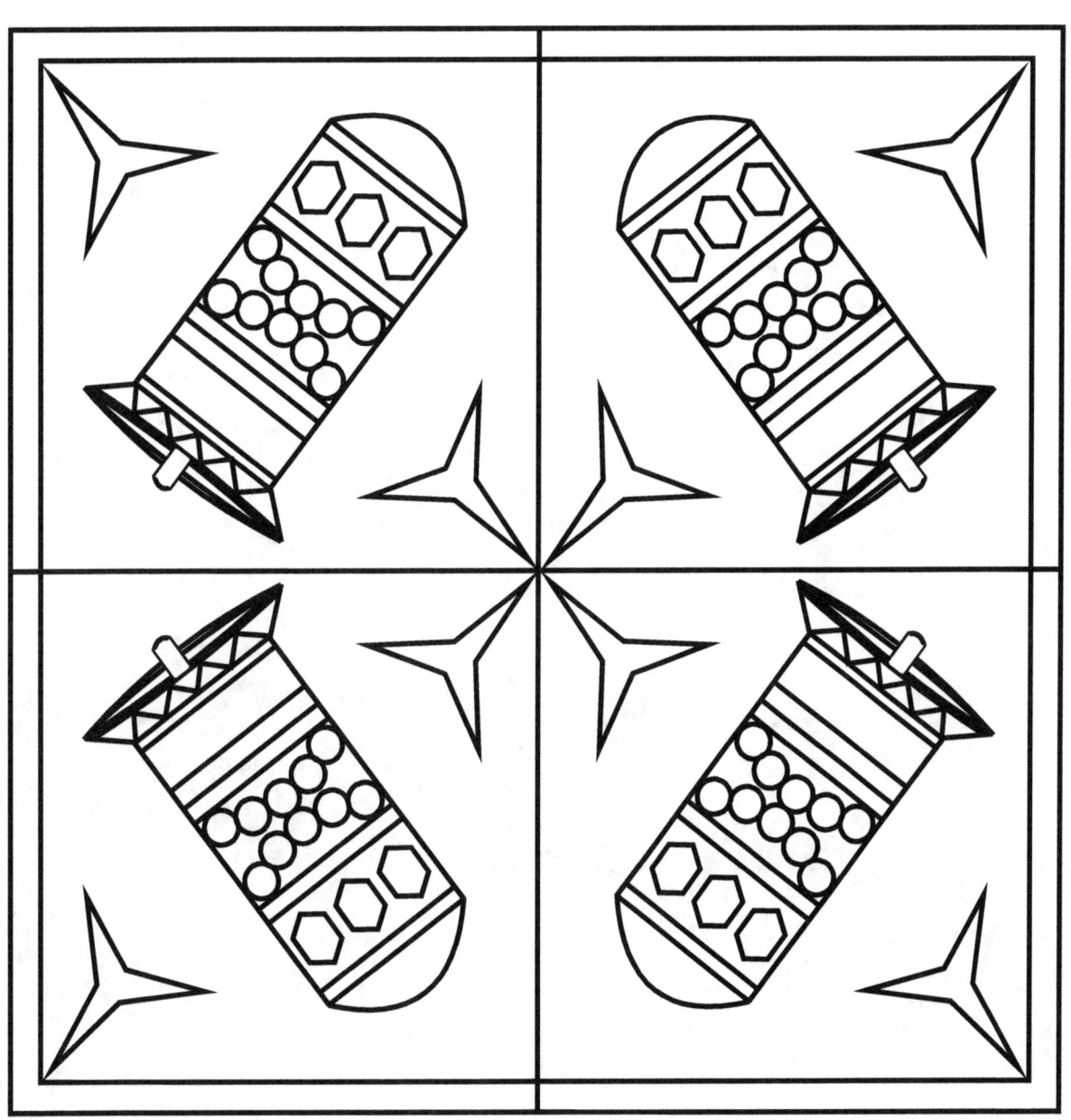

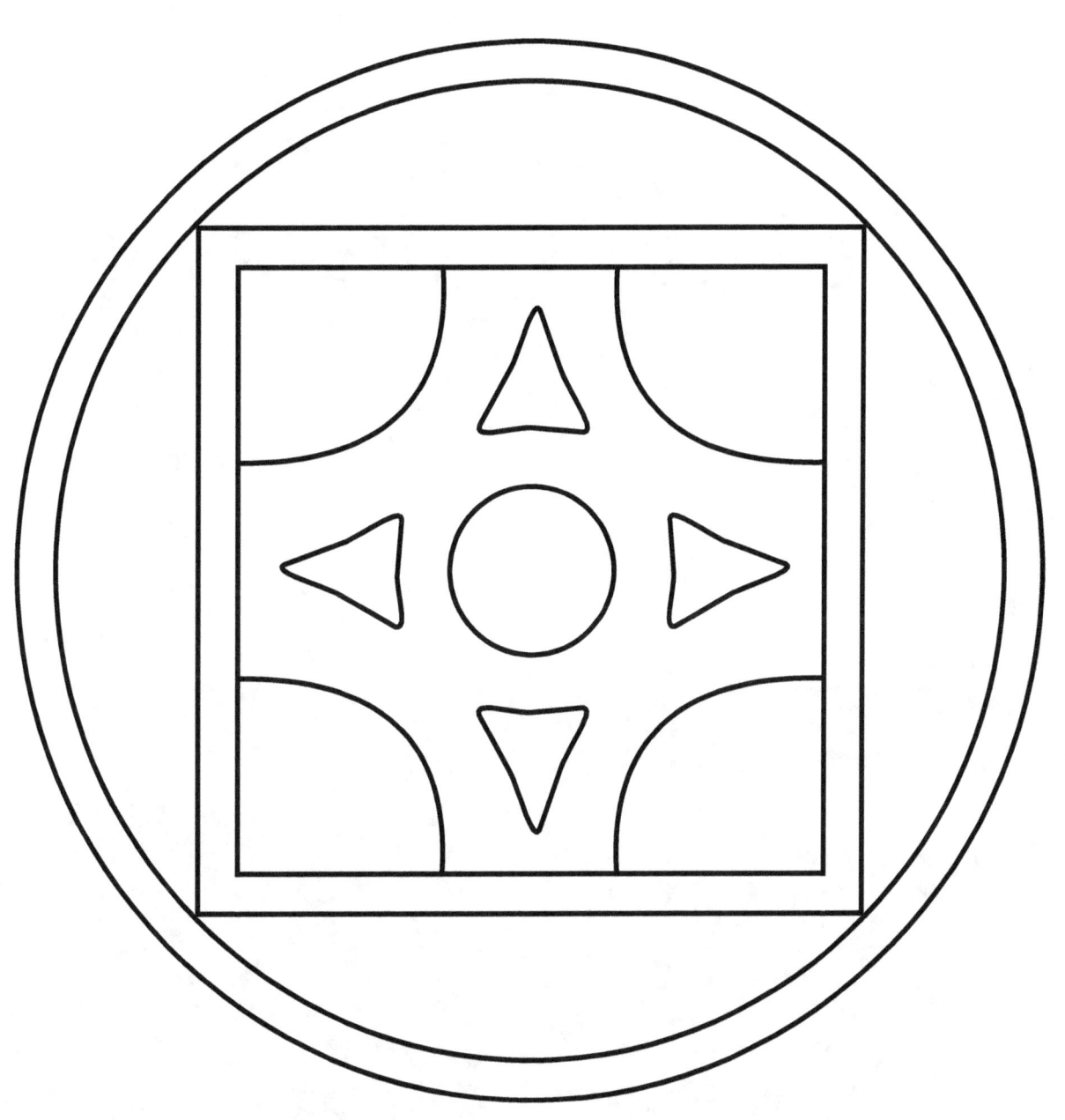

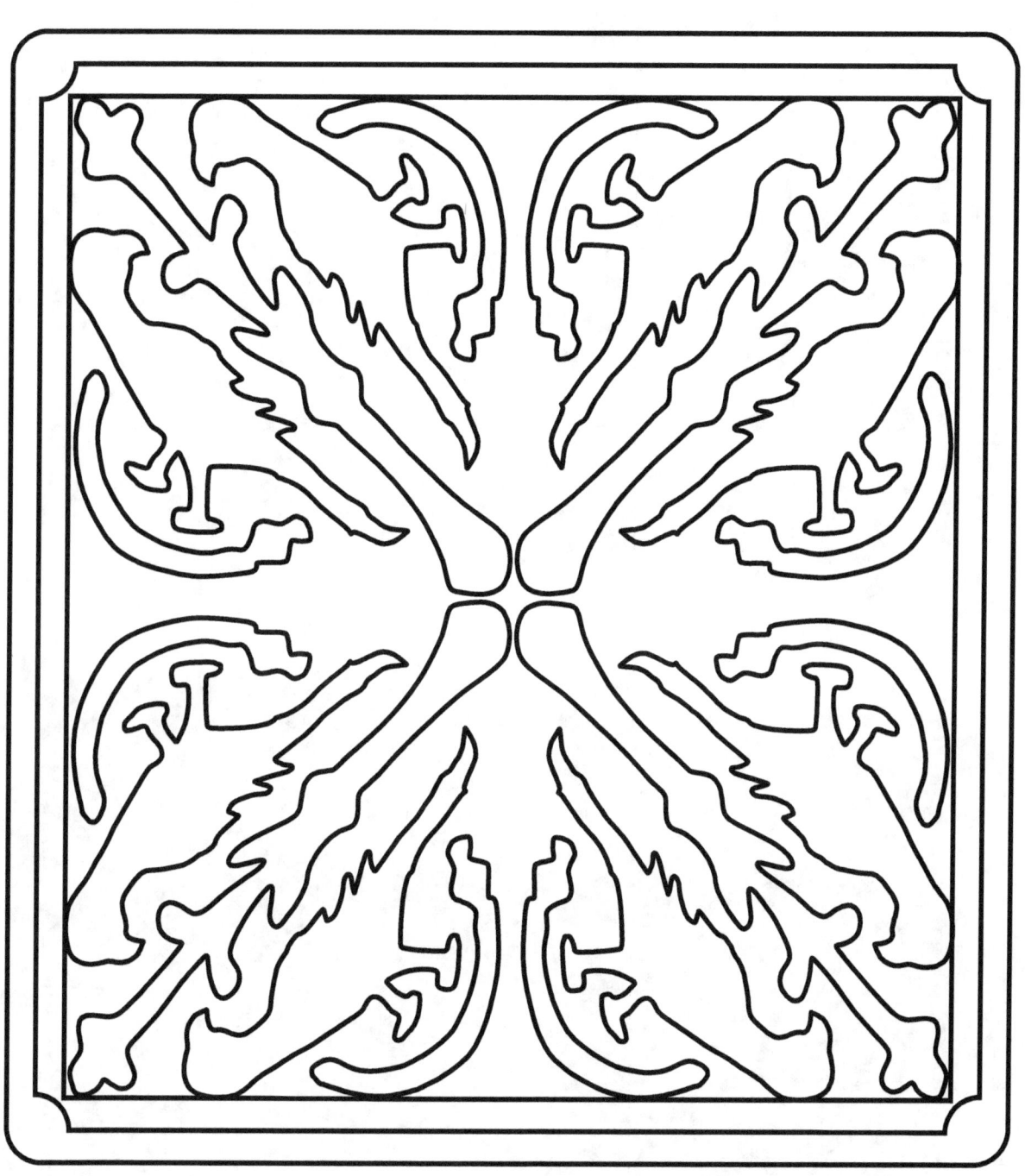

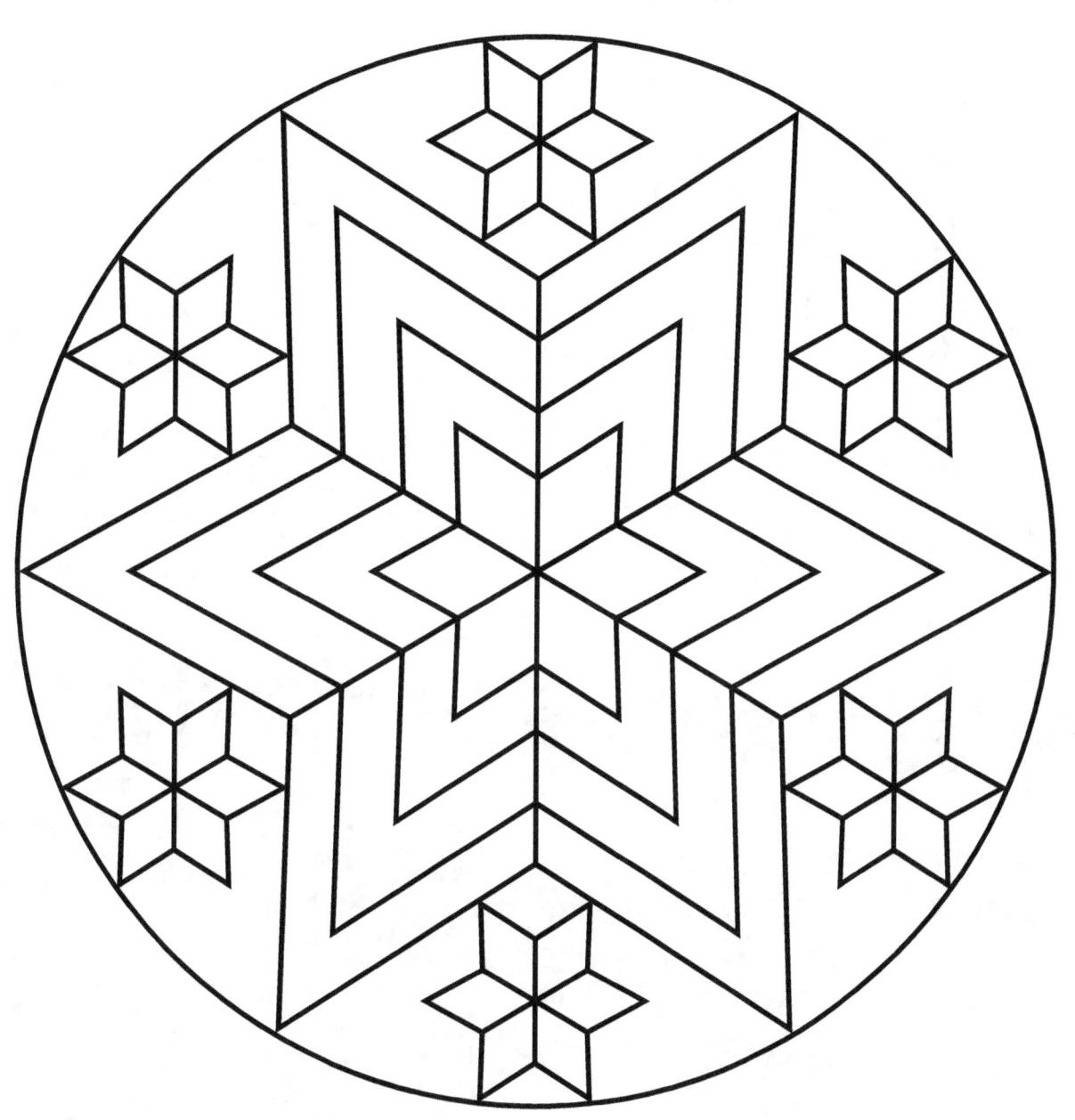

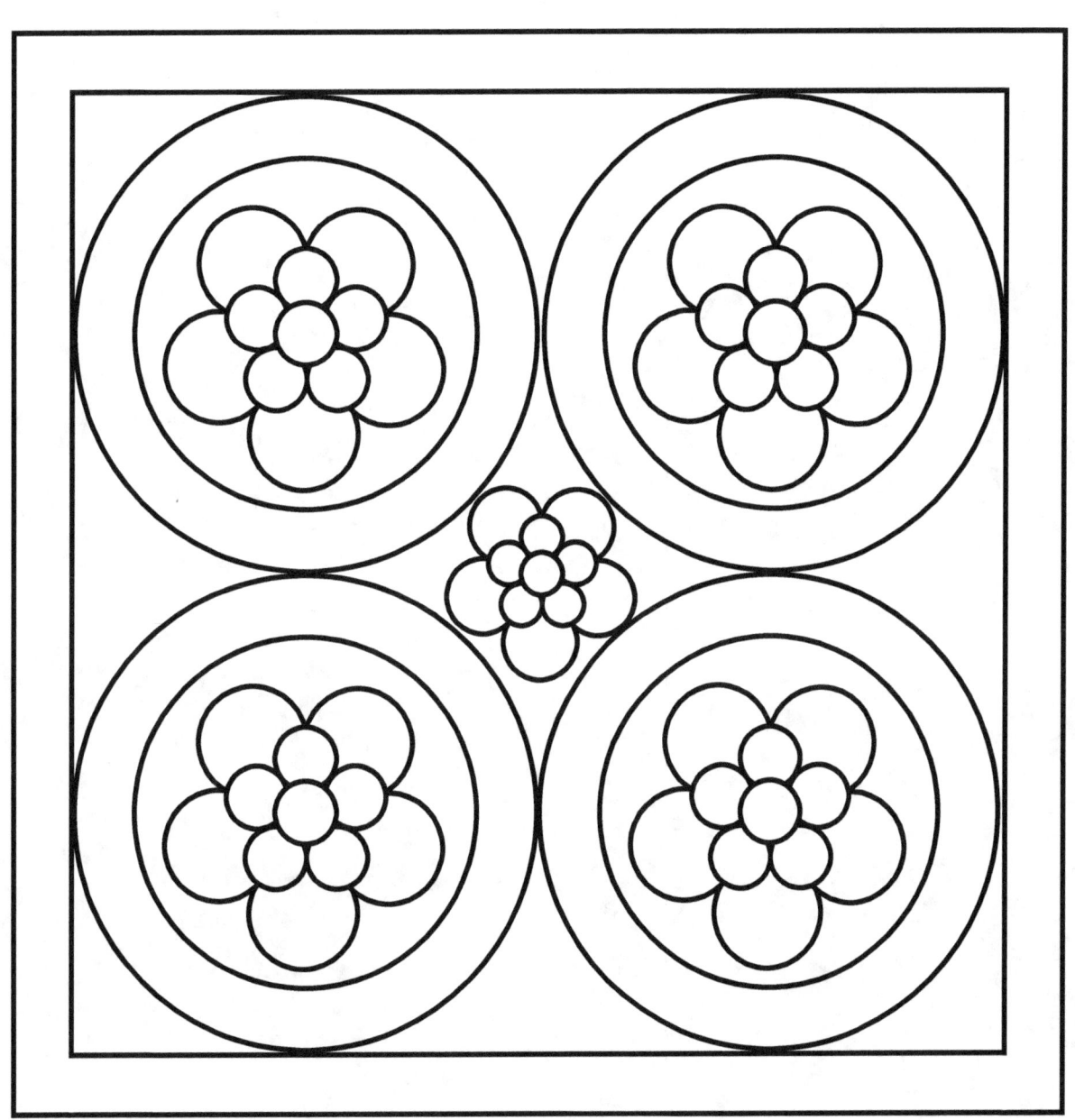

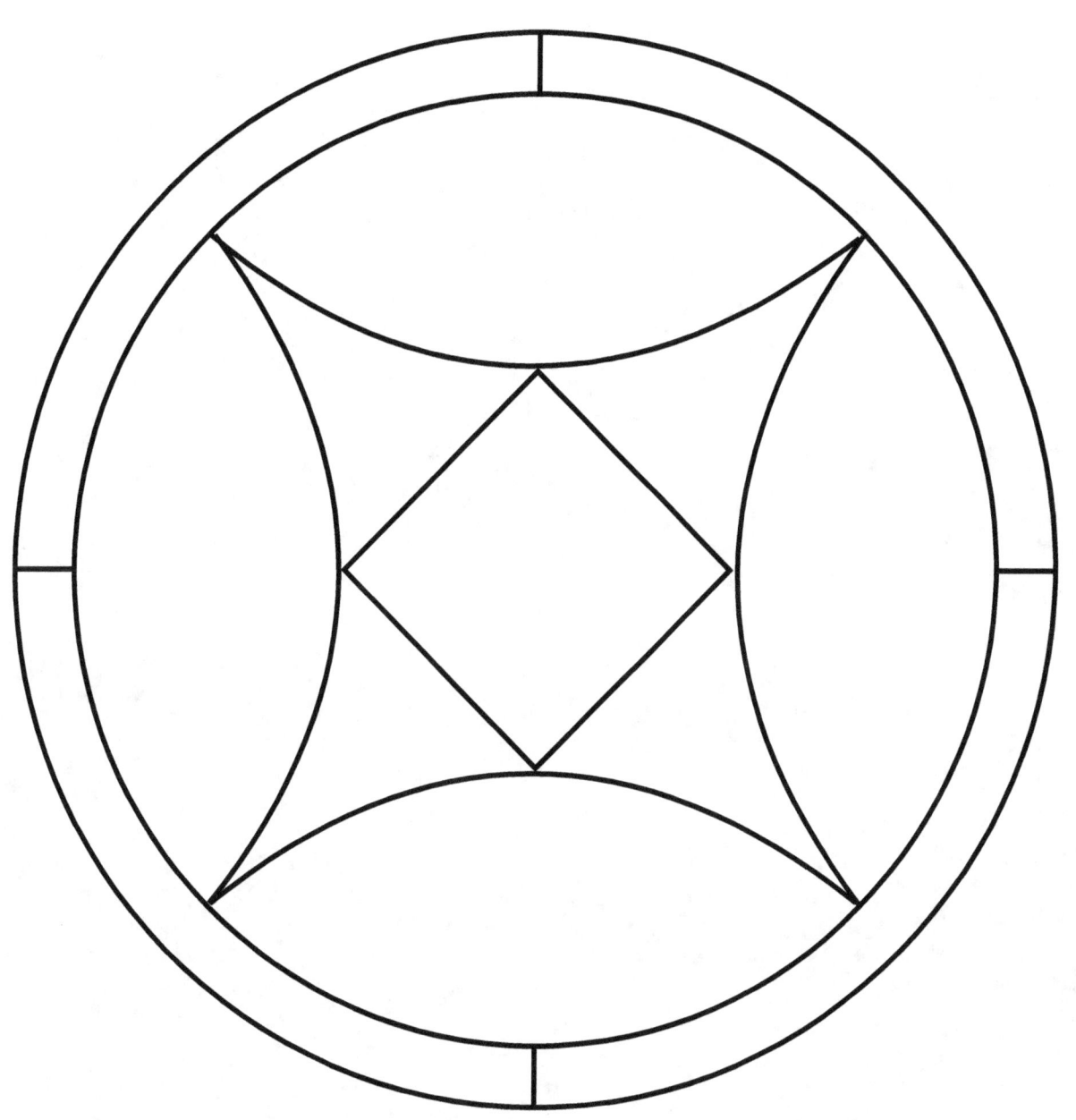

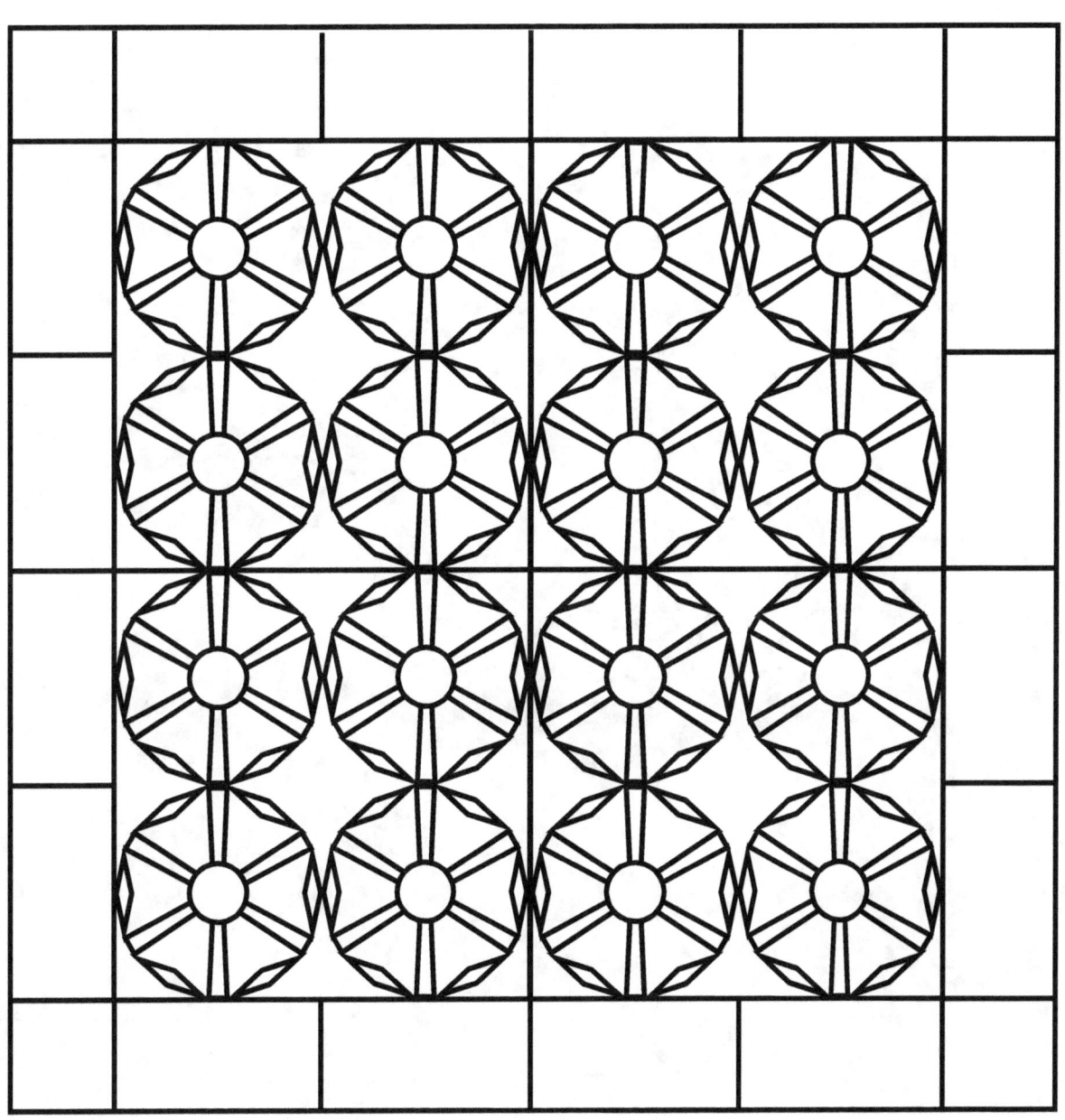

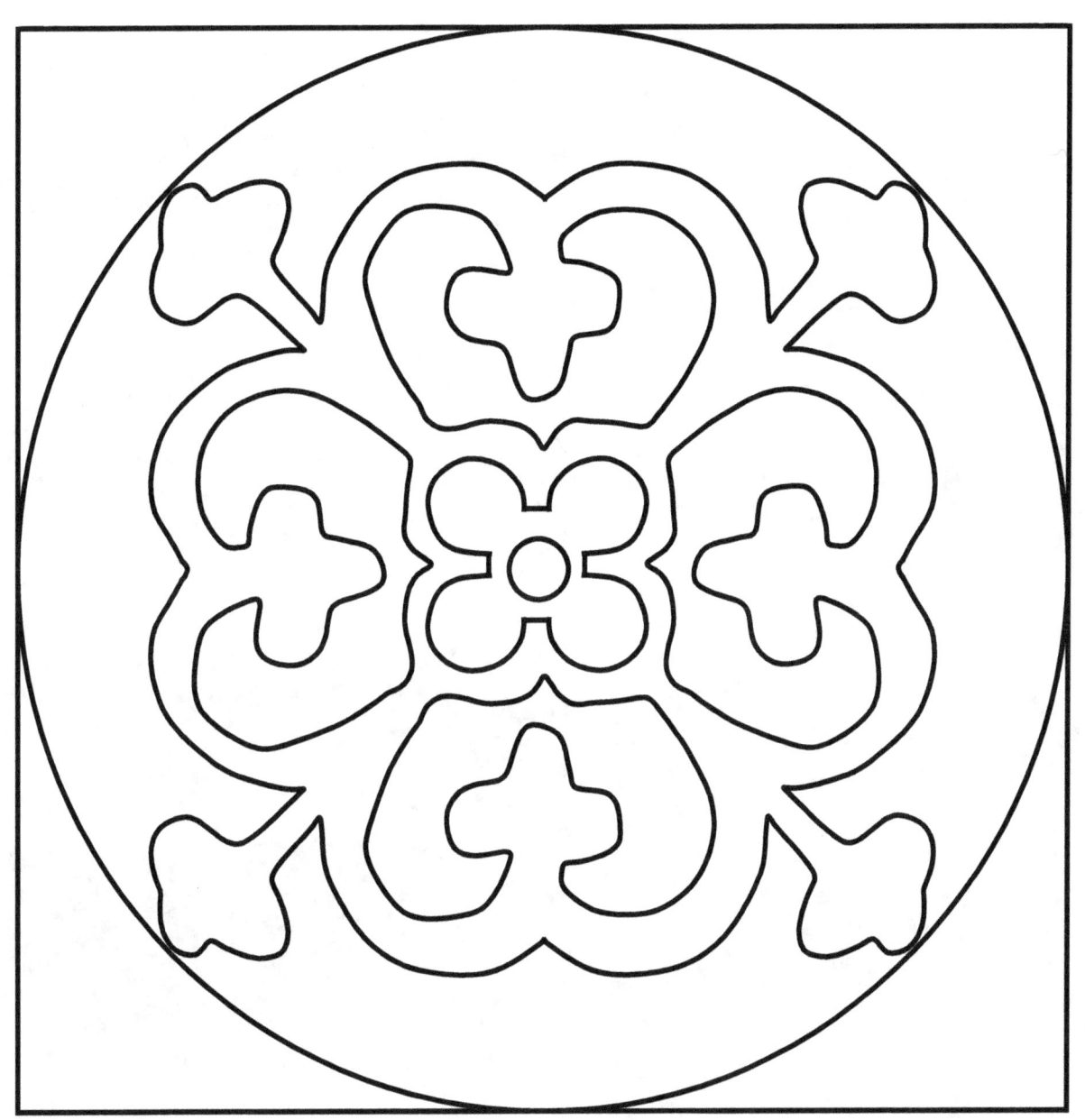

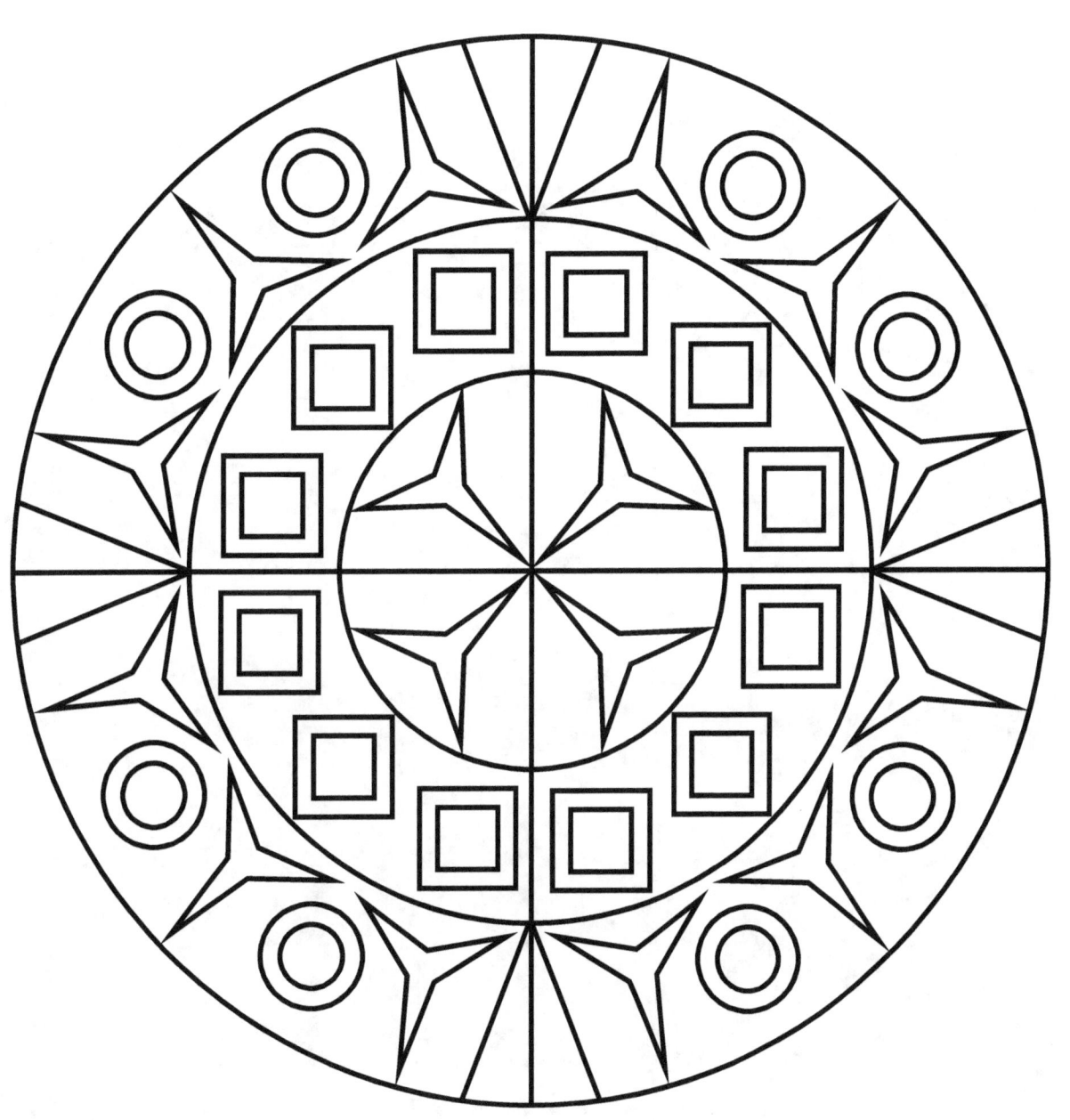

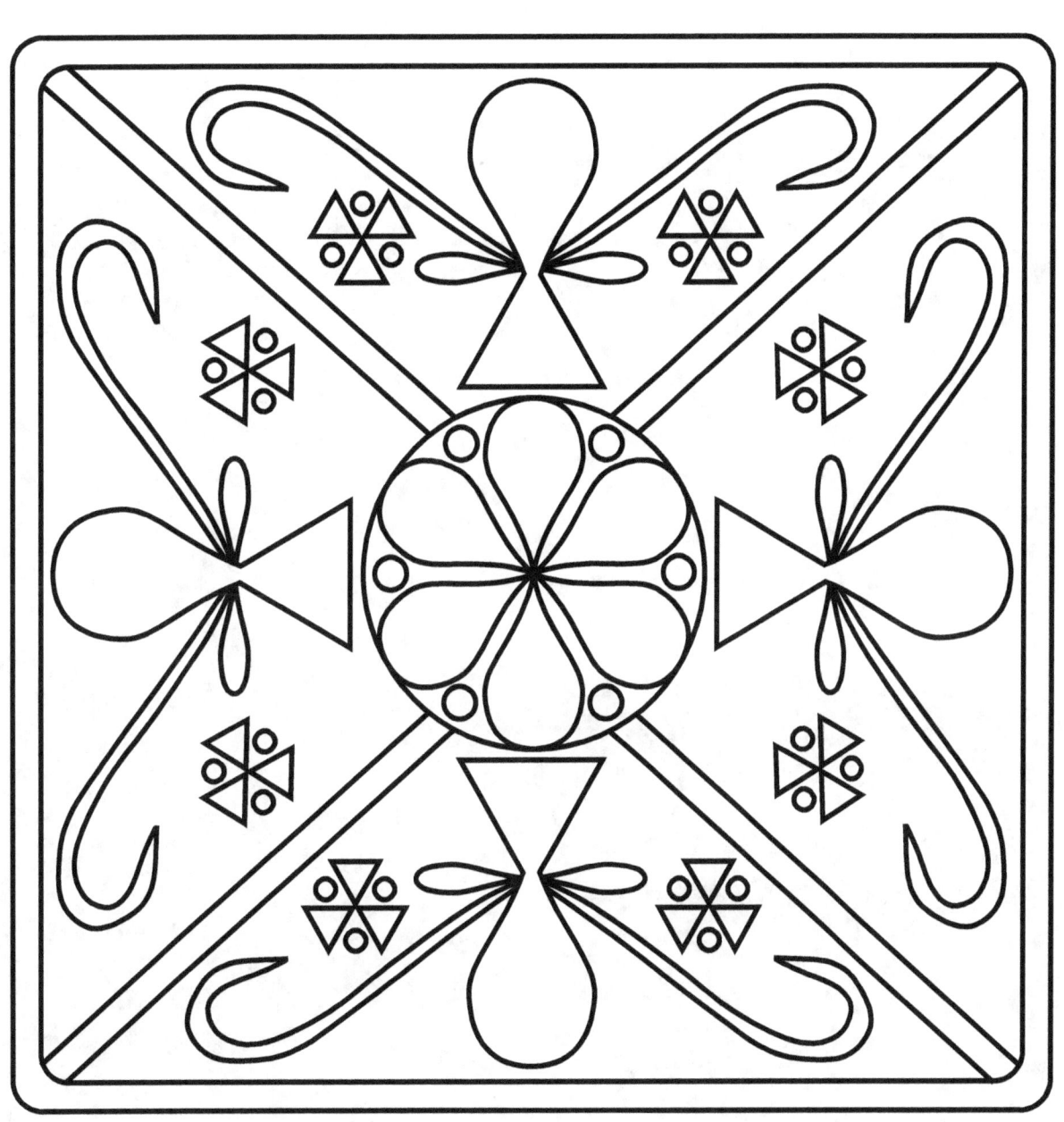

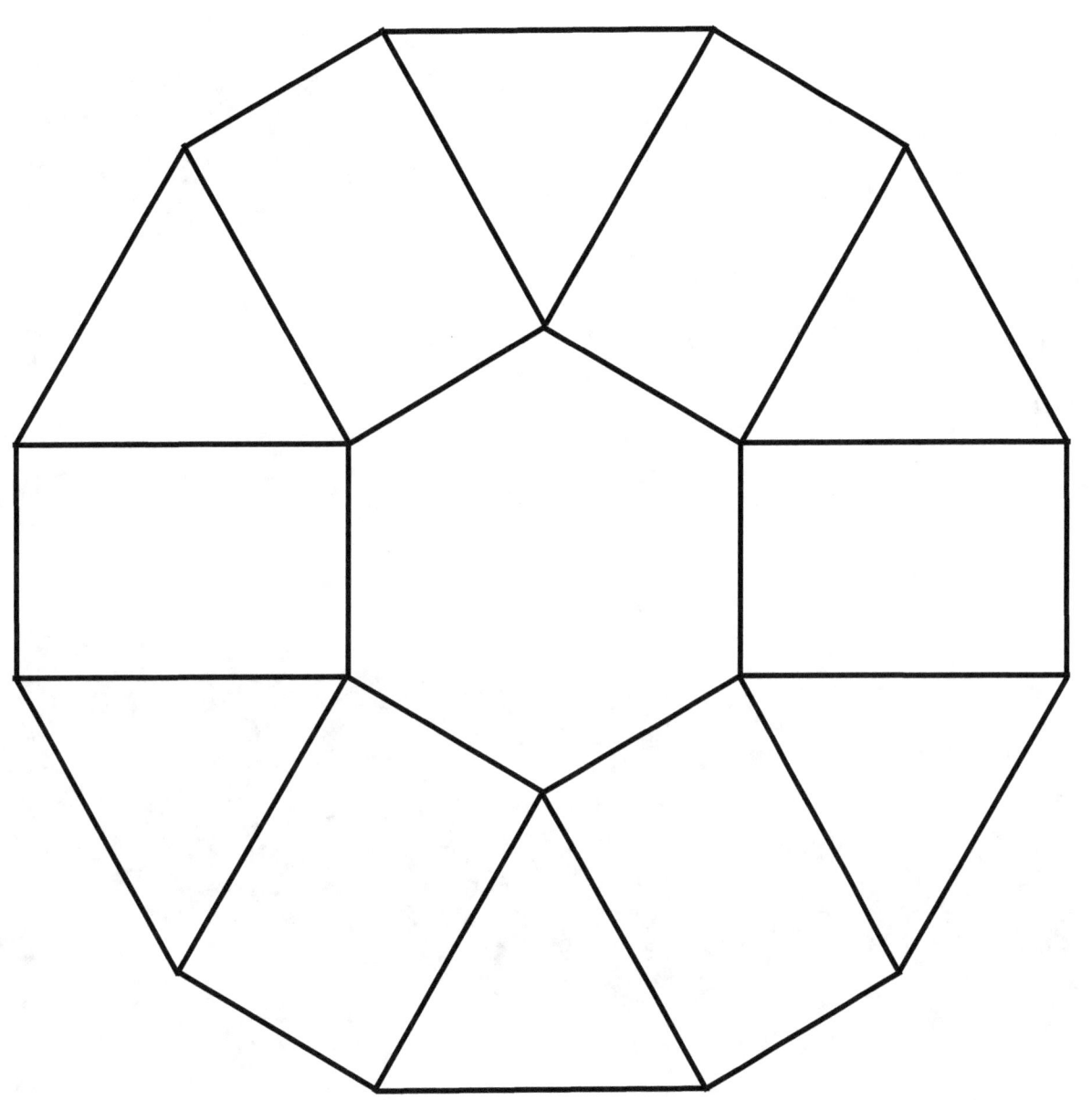

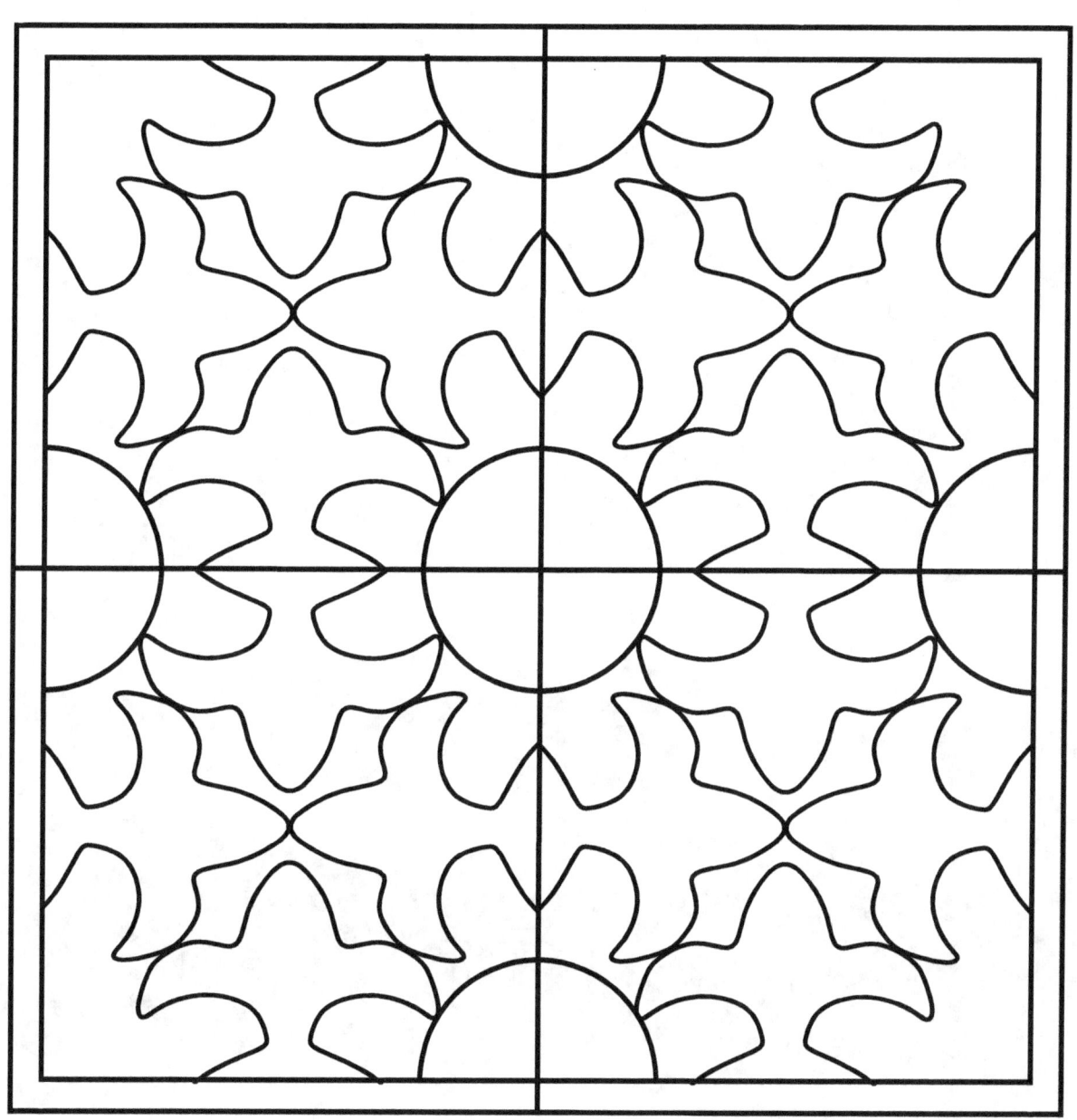

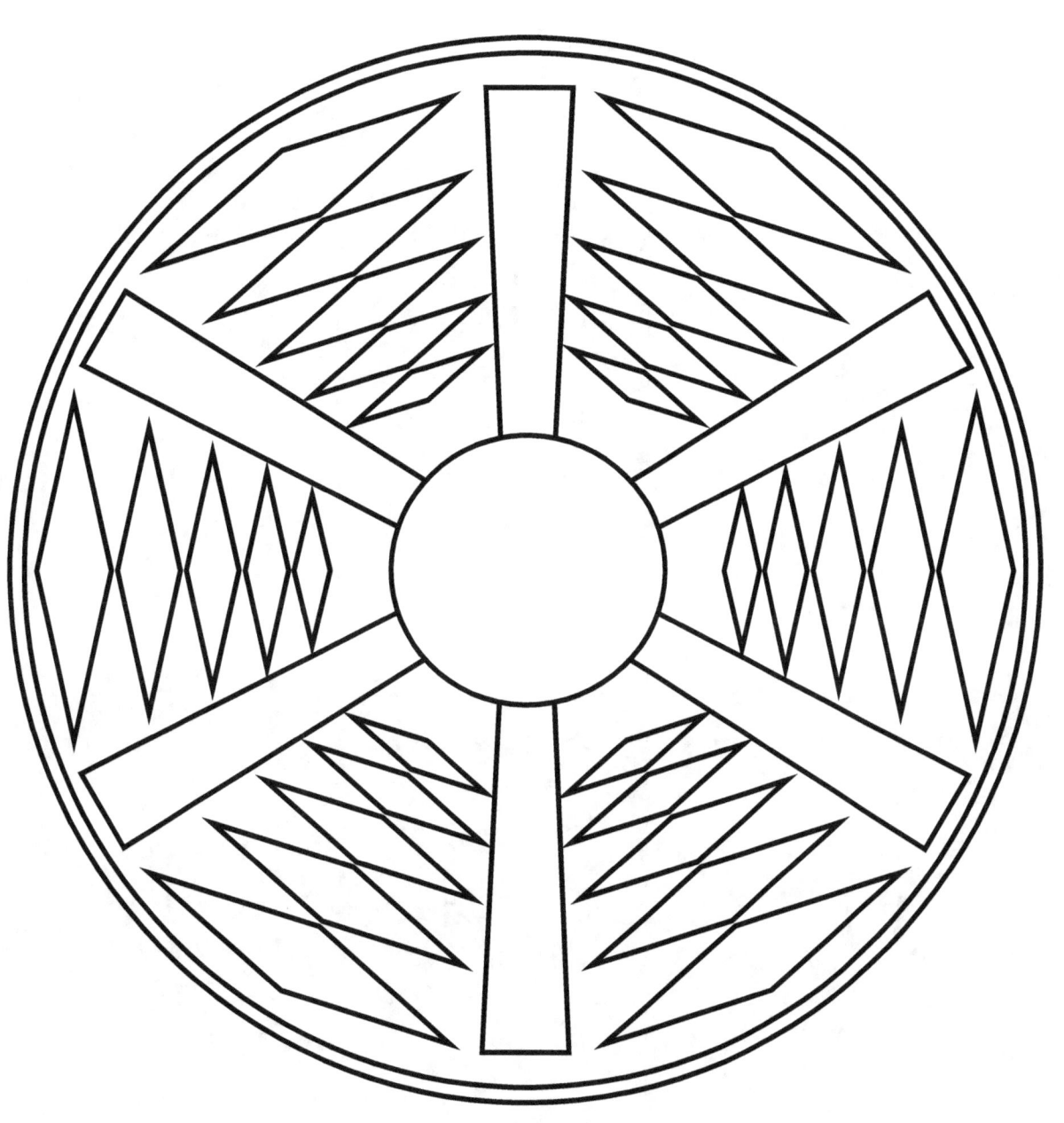

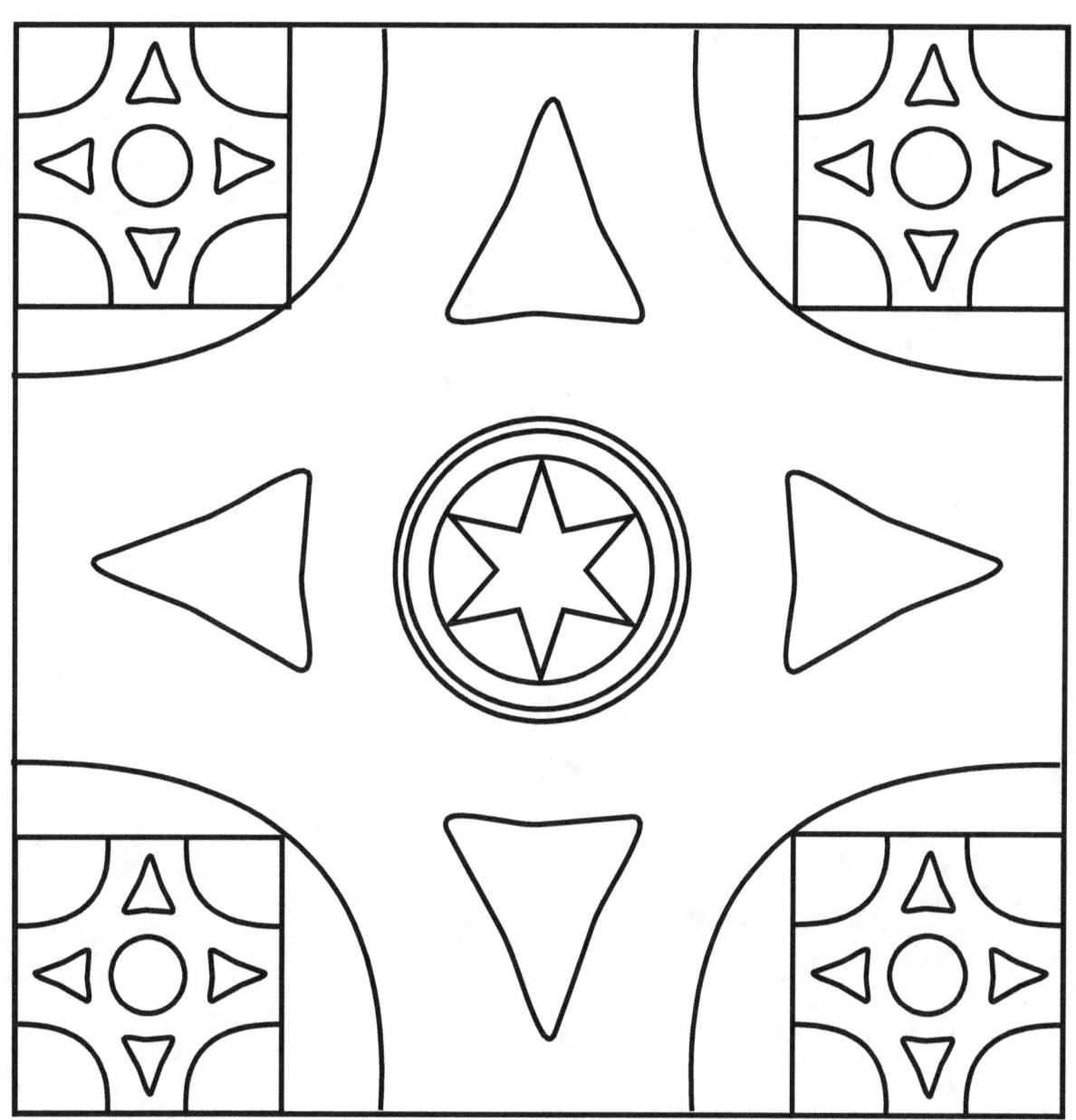

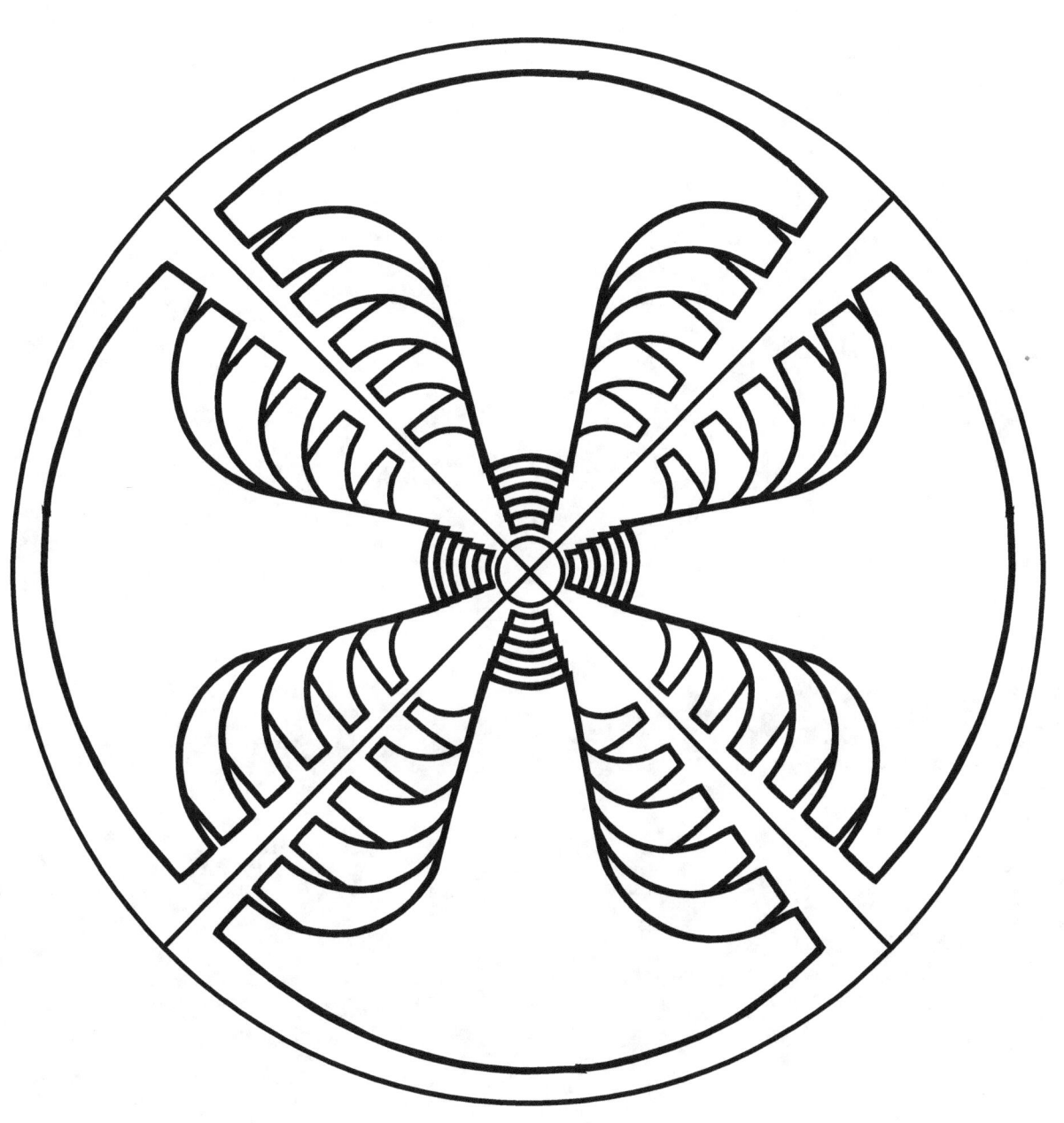

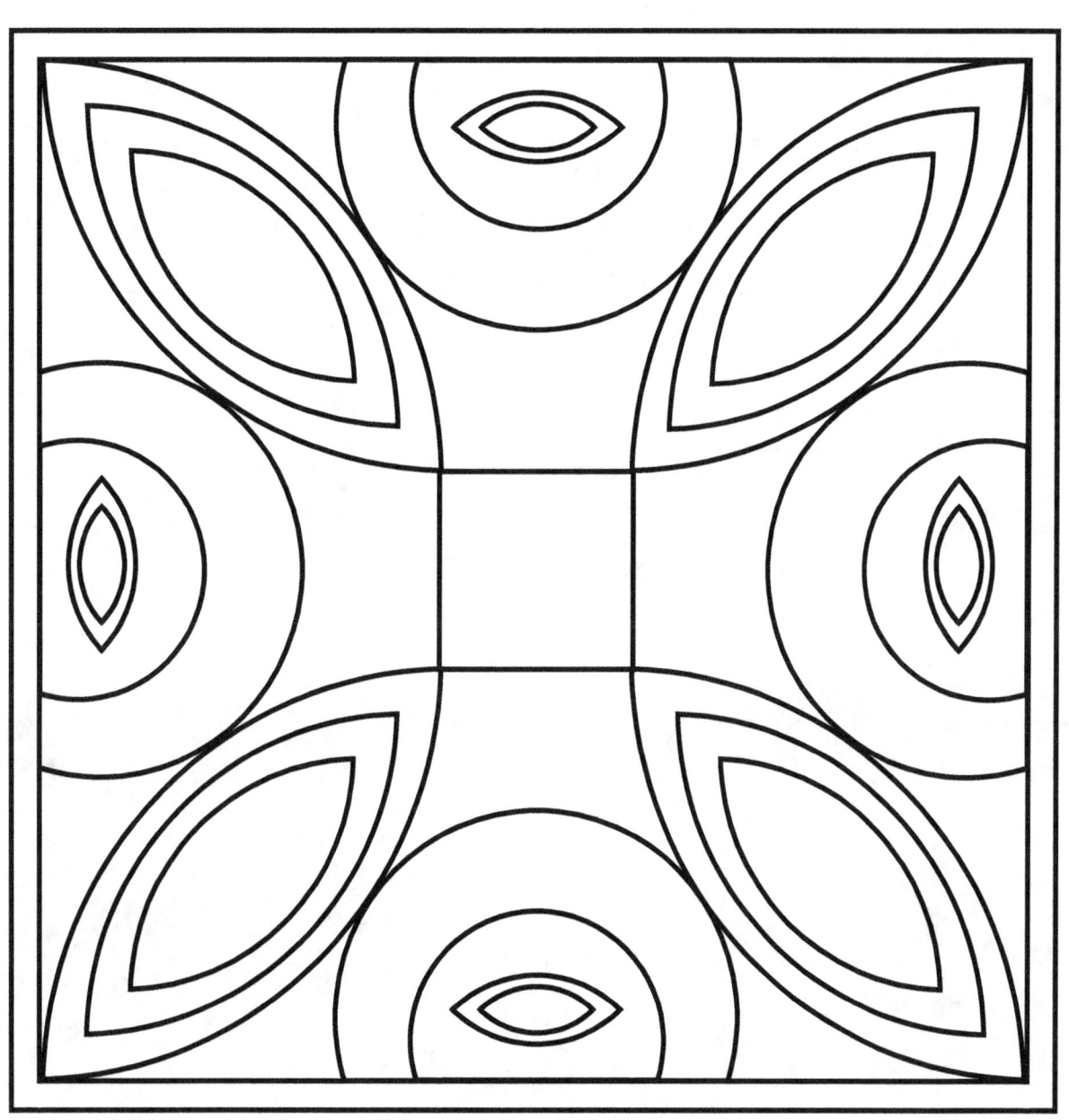

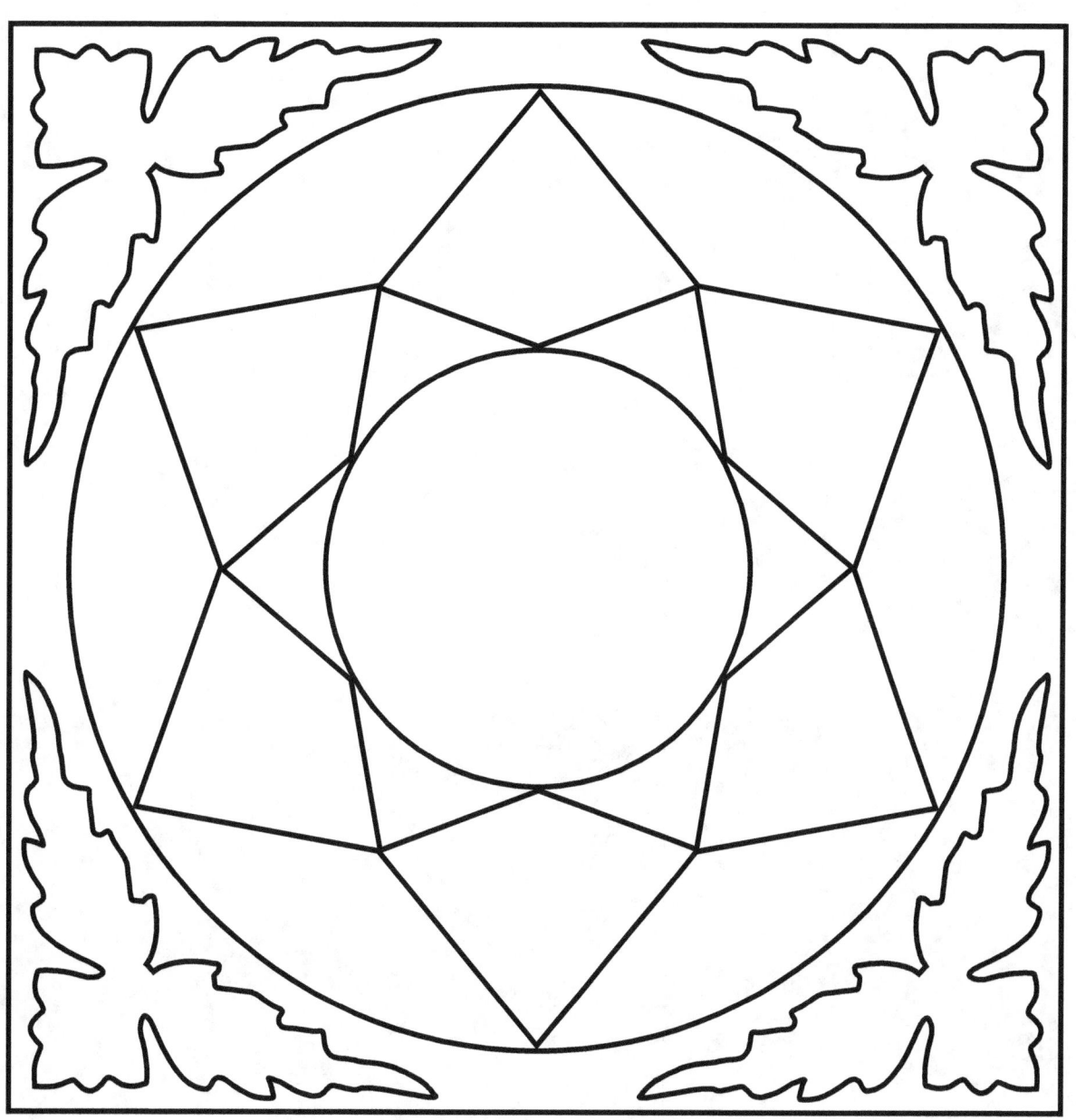

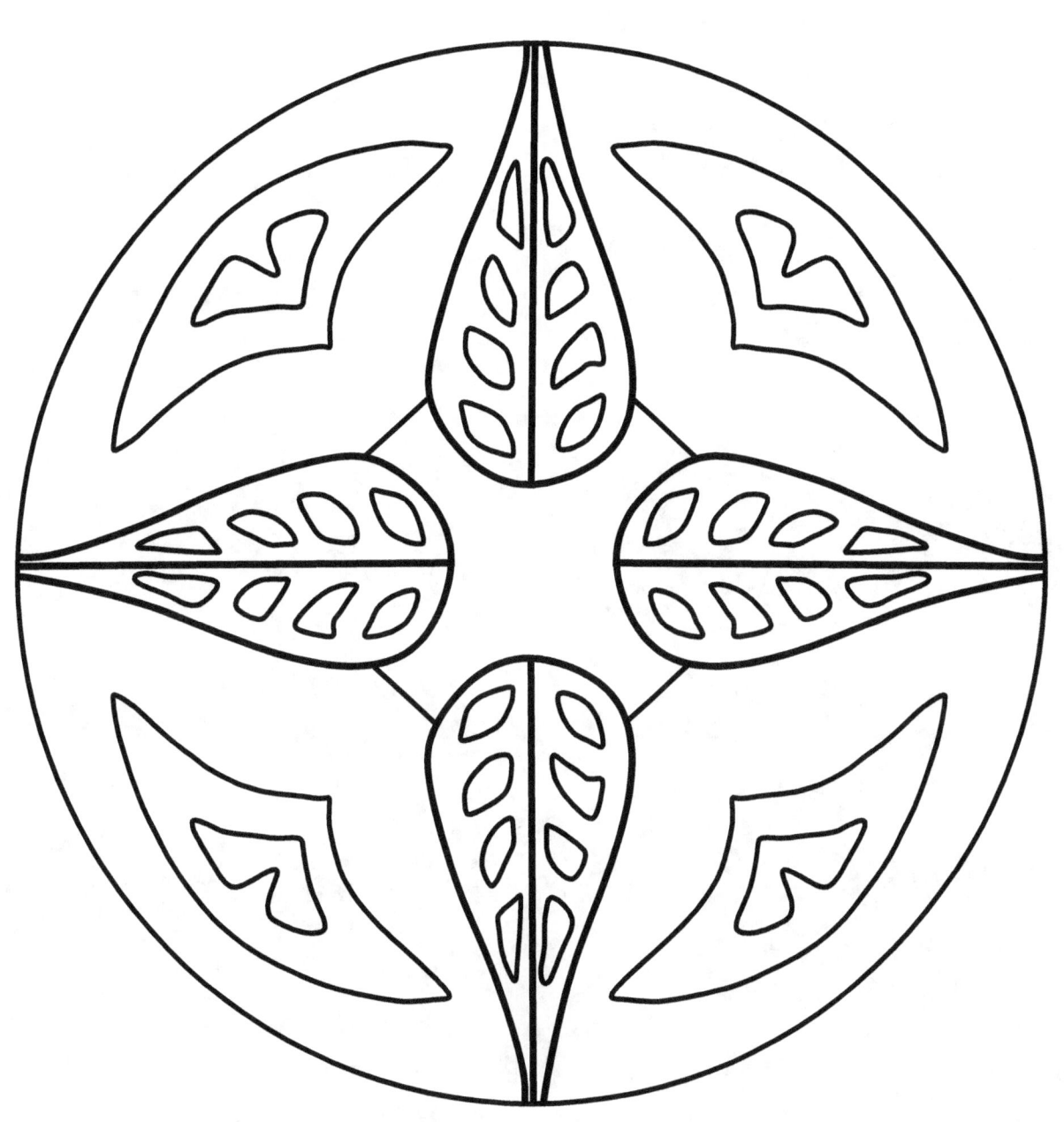

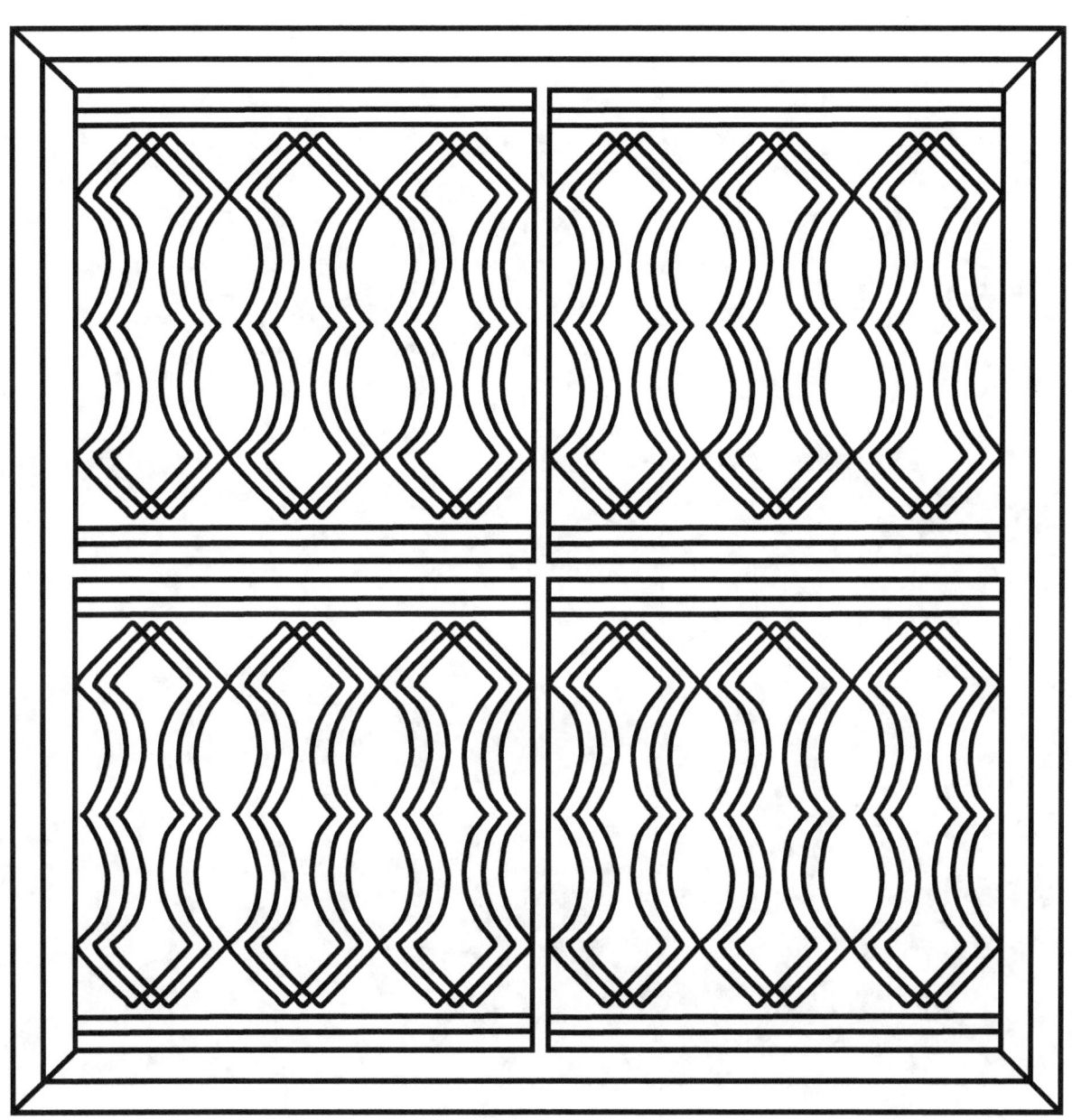

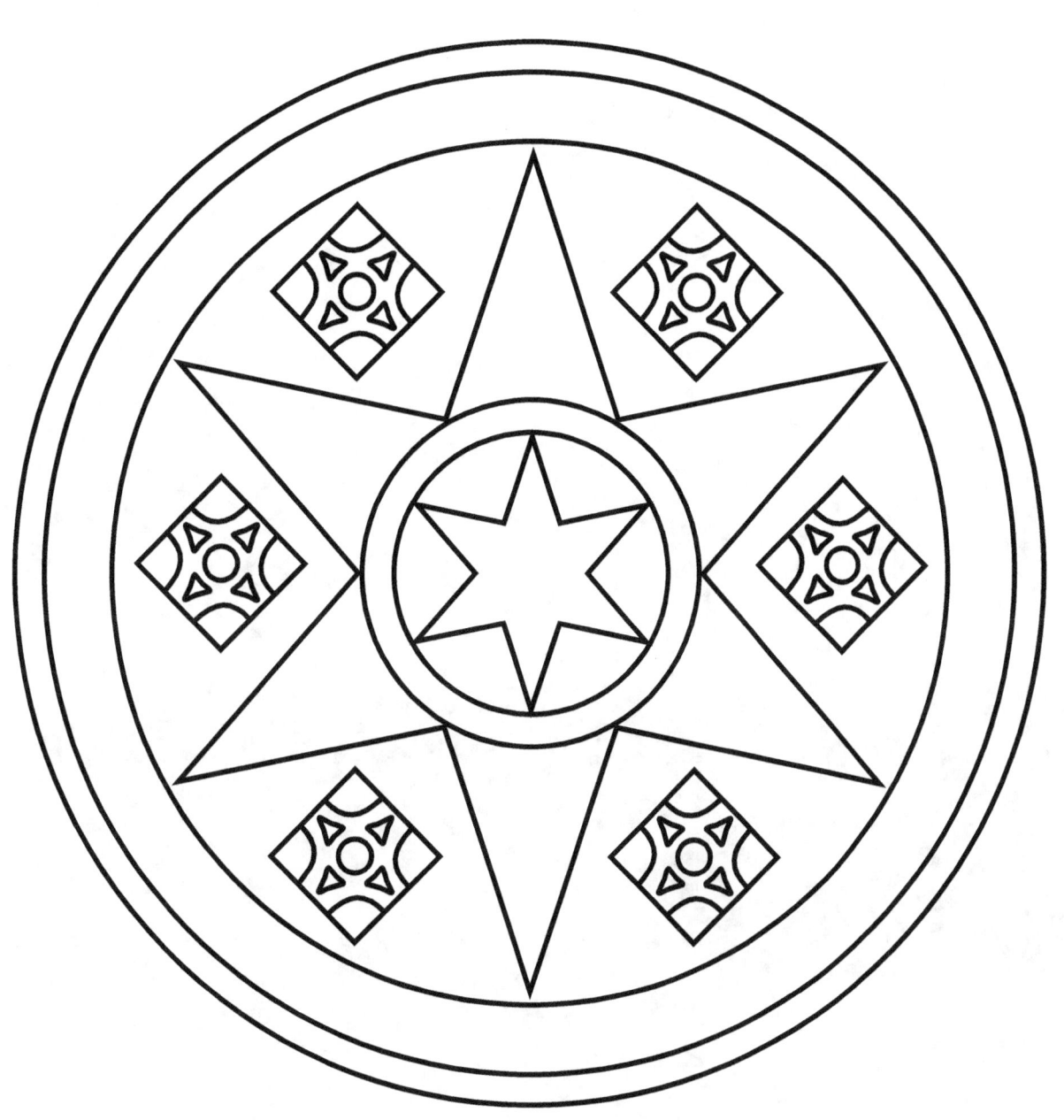

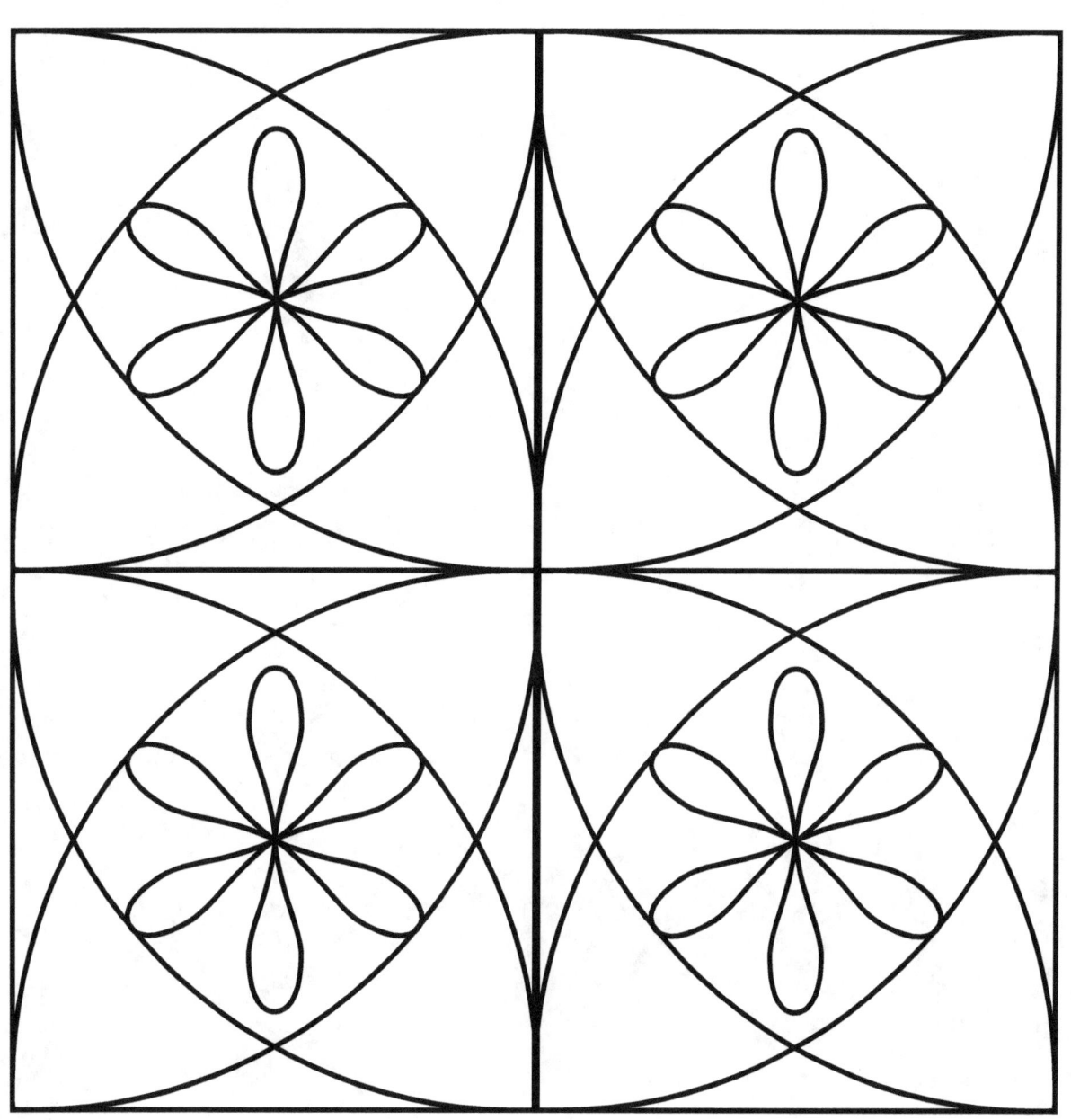

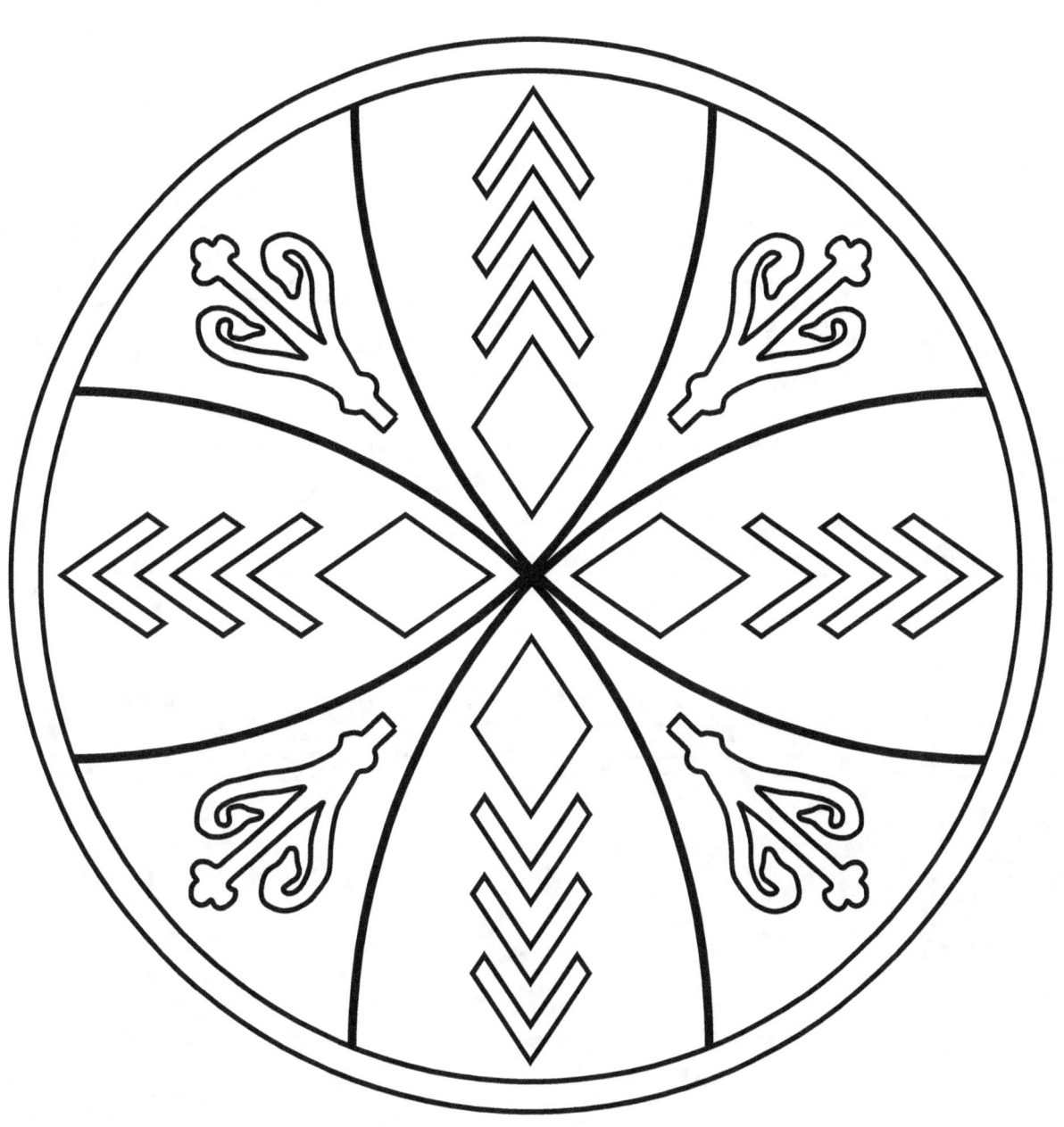

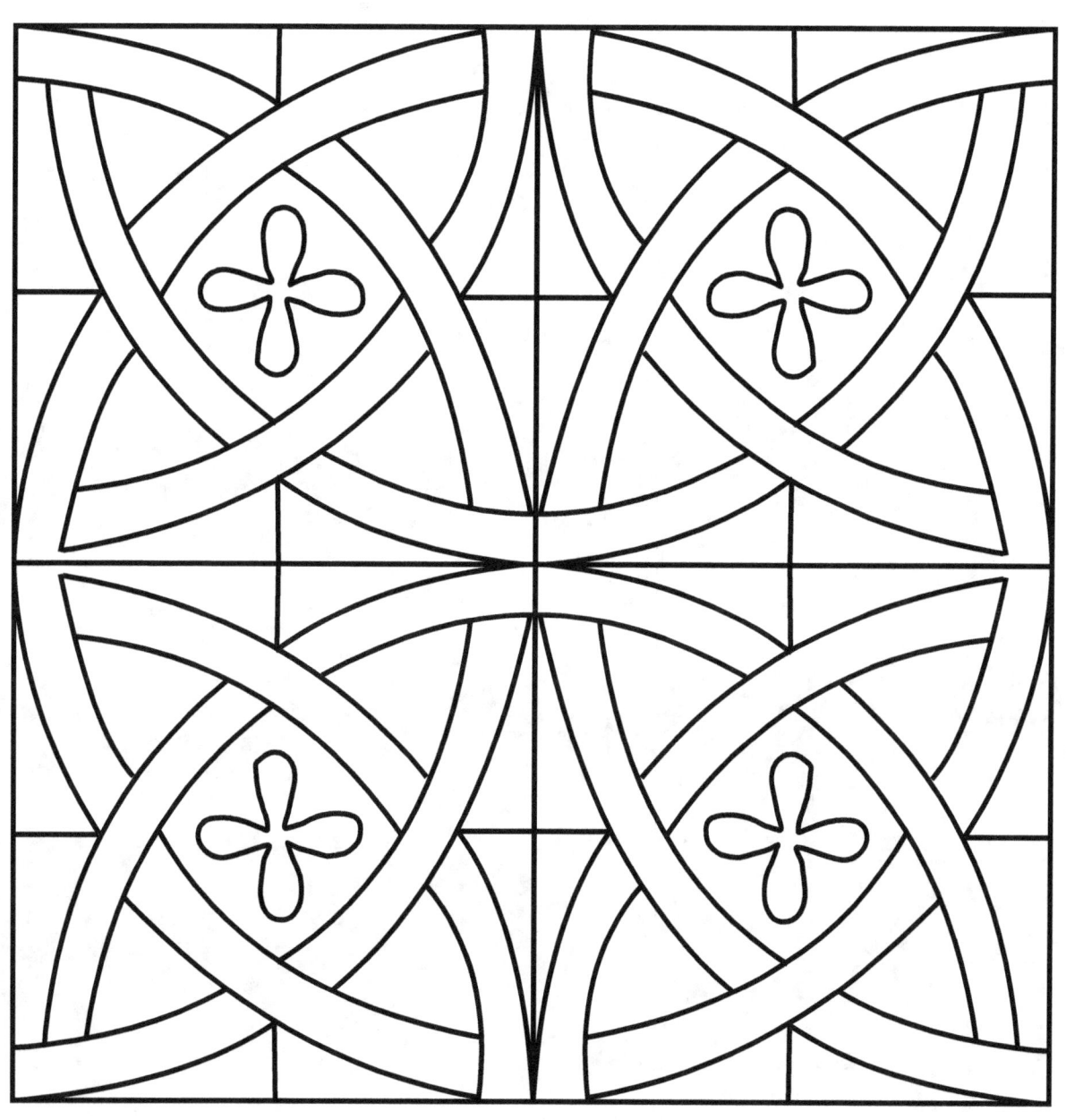

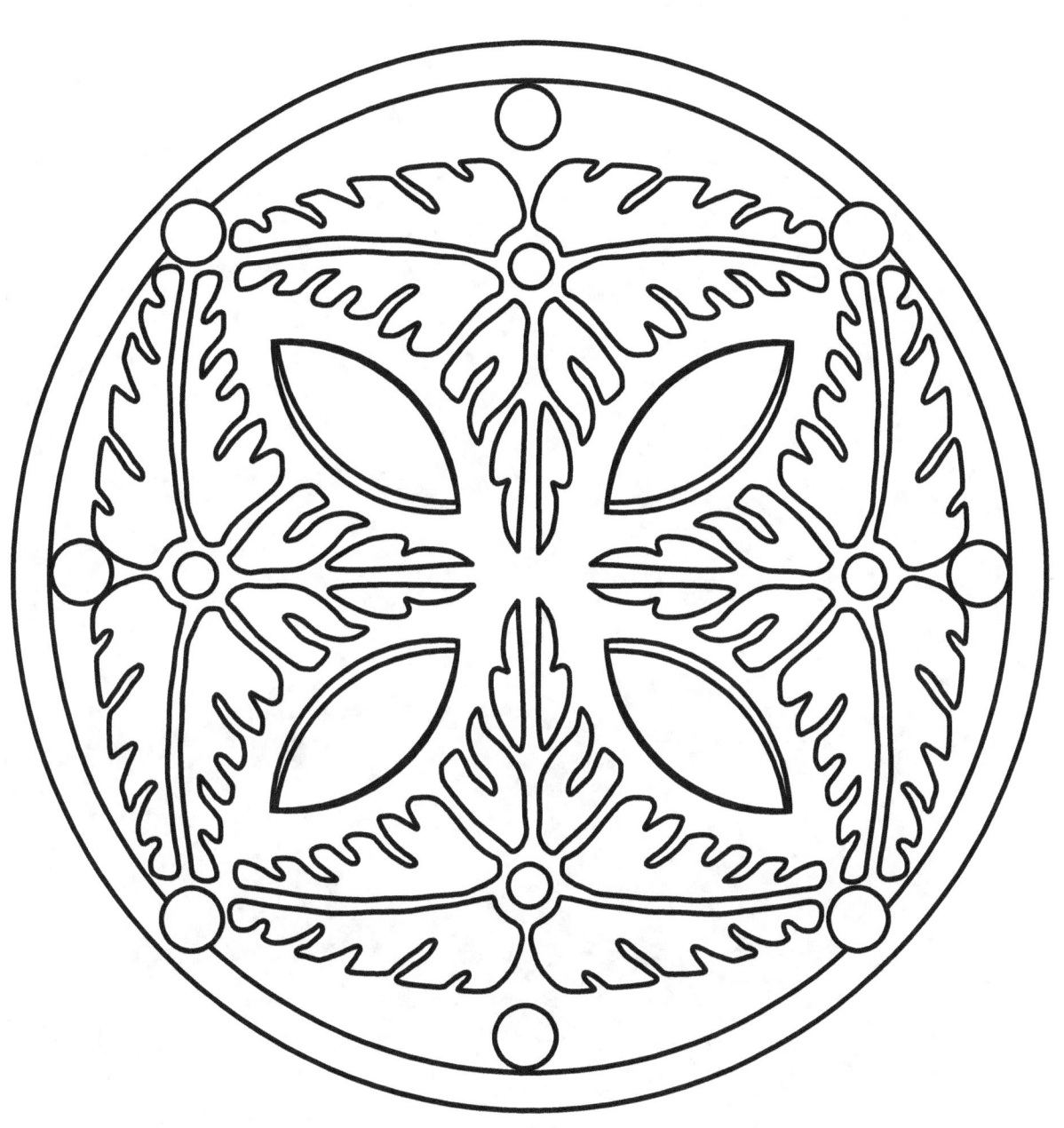

More colouring books can be found at

www.tigmorbooks.co.uk

www.ingramcontent.com/pod-product-compliance
Lightning Source LLC
Chambersburg PA
CBHW081749220526
45468CB00008B/2302